Foreign Policy Analysis

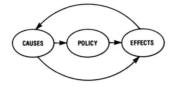

Policy Studies
Organization Series

Foreign Policy Analysis

Edited by
Richard L. Merritt
University of Illinois at
Urbana-Champaign

Lexington Books
D.C. Heath and Company
Lexington, Massachusetts
Toronto   London

Library of Congress Cataloging in Publication Data

Main entry under title:

Foreign policy analysis

Includes index.
1. International relations—Research—Addresses, essays, lec-
tures. I. Merritt, Richard L.
JX1291.F66   327'.07'2   75-27808
ISBN 0-669-00251-8

Published simultaneously in Canada

Printed in the United States of America

International Standard Book Number: 0-669-00251-8

Library of Congress Catalog Card Number: 75-27808

To
Ross N. Berkes
Norman R. Fertig
Paul E. Hadley

who gave me the chance
"to learn from those who can teach."
(Sophocles, *Antigone*)

Contents

Foreign Policy Analysis

1

Foreign Policy Analysis

Richard L. Merritt

Foreign policymaking is essentially the task of devising strategies that utilize a nation-state's capabilities to achieve the goals its leaders set. What the nation-state's capabilities are and how they are perceived, how decisionmakers mobilize these capabilities, who the individuals and groups that play significant roles are, what their patterns of interaction are, what they perceive their valued goals to be, how they seek to implement them, what international constraints foreclose some options and make the selection of others more likely—all these questions and more form the sometimes intractable core of concerns for both those who formulate foreign policies and those who analyze the policies developed.

Indeed, so broad is the range of questions important in the foreign policymaking process that no single volume can cover them all, least of all a collection of essays from different analysts, few of whom approach the topic from the same perspective. This volume,[a] then, presents not a rigorous, systematic, and complete analytic framework for the study of foreign policy, but rather some thoughts and current research that contribute to the development of such a framework.

Environments of Foreign Policy Decisionmakers

Constraints from the External Environment

The ecology of a national foreign policy decision system poses varying degrees of constraint upon its options and behavior. By this is meant not merely the physical environment, although clearly such factors as the worldwide distribution of resources and quality of life are important, too. Other constraints include the structure of the international system, varying levels of technology, enduring patterns of trade and other transactions,

---

[a] With two exceptions, the chapters in this volume are revisions of earlier papers prepared for a special issue of *Policy Studies Journal* 3:2 (Winter 1974); the other two were not finished in time for inclusion in the earlier publication. I am indebted to Stuart S. Nagel, journal coordinator of the Policy Studies Organization, for guidance in the preparation of both the special issue of PSJ and the present volume; and to Anna J. Merritt, who prepared the index for this volume.

perceptions, norms of individual and state behavior, and, more particularly, religion and other cultural components.

The first part of this volume deals with some of these ecological constraints on national foreign policy decision systems. Richard N. Swift ("Morality and Foreign Policy") focuses upon moral standards, which are to be sure individual in their origin but which can have systemic effects if they are widely accepted. He argues for policies that derive less from the putative imperatives of the collectivity, such as "national interest" or "national security," and more from the conscious desire to realize human, individual values such as the freedom and safety of individual human beings.

In his chapter on "Foreign Policy Outputs and International Law," Don C. Piper discusses the circumstances in which foreign policymakers adhere to the norms of international law or, should they perceive this adherence as endangering national interests, particularly national security, ignore or try, even unilaterally, to change the norms. The new rules they assert may pose some short-run destabilizing dangers (such as unwittingly setting undesired precedents) but, if generally accepted, may well contribute to the growth of the international legal order.

Aline O. Quester and George H. Quester ("You Can't Get There from Here") examine how policymakers transfer some traditional notions of the free market economy to foreign policy, including responses to ecological change. An "unresponsive" world arena, responding apparently idiosyncratically to normal pressures of the market place, can lead policymakers to rely excessively upon violence or the threat to use force, and revolution rather than compliance may be the unintended consequence.

Domestic Constraints

Another type of ecological constraint on foreign policymakers comprises other actors in the domestic political arena. What springs to mind most immediately, of course, is the plethora of interest groups making demands upon the decision system. Representatives of business, labor, ethnic associations, civic bodies, communications media, and still other aggregates who feel that a nation's foreign policy affects them may seek to voice their concerns and desires. Then, too, in certain, rather narrowly circumscribed circumstances, the public at large can have a direct impact upon the foreign policymaking process as well as, through its elected representatives and other mediators, a more indirect influence. What is sometimes forgotten in examining a decision system's internal environment is the fact that the very structure of that environment conditions the decisions made by the duly authorized decisionmaking bodies. A fragmented society, for instance, may pose vastly different considerations (such as freedom of action) than one that is highly mobilized and attuned to policy outcomes.

Part II of this volume examines some domestic constraints on foreign policy. Barry S. Rundquist and David E. Griffith ("The Parochial Constraint on Foreign Policymaking") consider why in principle foreign policymaking in Congress would be affected by the geographic distribution of military contracts in the United States. Kenneth Entin ("Legislator-Group Communications and Congressional Committee Decisionmaking"), using systematic interviews and questionnaires, focuses more directly upon how members of the House Armed Services Committee utilize information from lobbyists, and how the latter seek to influence the Committee members to adopt particular measures. "The Role of the Opposition in Foreign Policymaking," writes Sheldon Appleton, can sometimes be considerable. In making policy, an elected leader may modify his behavior to respond to the anticipated reaction of the opposition (both inside or outside his own party), or else undercut the opposition's strength by appropriating their policies and enunciating them as his own.

Implications for Policy Studies

Implicit in all these chapters is the proposition that decisionmakers' cognitive processes mediate the "reality" of the environmental constraints, whether external or domestic. When national leaders look at their decisionmaking ecology, they may see widely variant realities. Adolf Hitler saw weak liberal democracies in the West that would yield to German demands rather than incur the risk of war; and his imagery endowed the German people with a "will" that could overcome any obstacle. A generation later, American policymakers perceived the North Vietnamese to be as soft as U.S. resources were limitless.

In some cases, perceptions of an environment act as self-fulfilling prophecies. Belief in an hostile environment may lead decisionmakers to prepare their defenses and take advantage of the weaknesses of other states—thereby themselves contributing significantly to the level of hostility in the world arena. Similarly, a population confident that it can defeat its foe may well conduct warfare with an élan that makes up for moderate deficiencies in its resource endowment.

In other cases, however, such perceptions produce tragic consequences, both for those holding them and others with whom they come into contact. The views of Hitler and the Johnson administration were both correct—up to a point. Ultimately their policies, filled with elements of fantasy, crashed into the barriers of a concrete reality that frustrated their dreams, just as most individuals who persuade themselves that they can fly find themselves in trouble when they leap from a twentieth-floor window. It is not merely perceptions of the external world and one's own capabilities, then, that count. Matching these perceptions with empirical referents from the real world is also important.

A critical task for foreign policy analysis is to improve the ability of decisionmakers to ascertain both the manifold aspects of their environment and the appropriateness of particular policies for dealing with them. Injunctions to "see things more clearly" or "use all your analytic skills" or "think" are insufficient. Policy analysts can rather (1) generate propositions about the sources and consequences of perceptual behaviors, (2) elaborate existing techniques and develop new ones that use systematic data to evaluate key aspects of international relations and domestic capabilities, (3) undertake empirical studies to validate these techniques, and (4) formulate explanatory models that integrate relevant data.

Important work in these directions is already well under way. In some areas, such as public opinion analysis, it is quite advanced. In others, such techniques as content analysis and interviews with policymakers show promise, however unwieldy they may be at present. And, of course, systematic thinking about how decisionmakers can use data and conceptual models to improve their performance stands at the heart of many current analyses of the foreign policy process.

Foreign Policy Process

In the foreign policy process, decisionmakers are not constrained solely by the demands made upon them by individuals and groups in their own country who want to see particular values maximized or even by the pressures and realities of the external environment. They also operate within a decision system that has its own dynamics. At the center of it stands a bureaucracy, a major function of which is to process relevant information from the external and domestic environments as well as that stored within the bureaucracy itself—to bring it to bear upon a current issue. Even more central is the fact that decisions are made by individuals, each with a distinctive personality. The interplay of the personalities of decisionmakers, group dynamics as decisionmakers interact, representative processes in the sense that top-level decisionmakers are tied into different bureaucracies and other social groupings, and the qualities of the information-processing system determines the issues to which foreign policymakers pay attention and the goals they pursue in the international arena.

Models and Research

A third part of this volume turns more directly to the analysis of the foreign policy process. Elmer Plischke, focusing upon the "Intellectual Dimensions of Foreign Relations Decisionmaking," sets out a broad analytic scheme for viewing the "cosmography" of decisionmakers. Particular attention is paid to the relative merits of advocacy and options analysis as procedures for determining policy. The latter, he concludes, by encouraging the creation and continued use of an integrated intellectual framework for considering options, may lead to a more consistent policy—that is less subject to fads, short-lived majorities, or the persuasiveness of particular advocates.

Stephen J. Cimbala, in his chapter on "Priorities and Limits in Studying Foreign Policy," points to the role of transdisciplinary behavioral science in establishing a conceptual and methodological core for analyzing foreign policy. He is especially interested in the interaction of "social facts" engendered by policy studies—that is, their descriptive, explanatory, and predictive findings—with decisionmakers' conceptual models in producing foreign policy.

A substantially different approach to foreign policymaking views it in the broader context of the international political system. "Events analysis," as it is frequently termed, tabulates the frequency and covariation of certain kinds of events either befalling a nation-state (revolutions, peaceful changes of government) or characterizing relationships between two countries (wars, threats, diplomatic recognition). To date, most such studies have held constant the main variables describing the decision process itself—personality factors, group dynamics, representational processes, information-processing systems—in concentrating upon patterns of systemic interaction. There is no inherent reason, however, why such studies in the future could not develop appropriate indicators of such variables, aggregated for each nation-state as a unit.

In their examination of events analyses, "Reconceptualizing Foreign Policy Behavior: The Problem of Discrete Events in a Continuous World," Jerry B. Jenkins and William O. Chittick point to another correctable problem. Such analyses to date have tended to view events as discrete, as separable analytically and hence separated from their context of an ongoing sequence of international interactions. While recognizing the analytic need to categorize, Jenkins and Chittick argue that only by reintroducing the patterns of events into their contextual frame of time and interaction can the approach truly be useful for policy analysts and policymakers who want to understand in a stochastic sense the full dimensions of international interaction.

Information and Actors

Another set of chapters examines more specific aspects of the foreign policy process. Two look at constraints on information flows within a foreign policymaking system. In the first of these, Thomas H. Karas sees "Secrecy as a Reducer of Learning Capacity in the U.S. Foreign Policy Bureaucracy." Overemphasis on secrecy may lead policymakers to ignore external criticism of the philosophic assumptions and perceptions that underlie their considerations, place a heavy burden on organizational resources, restrict the participation of potentially useful experts, and generate conflict within the foreign policymaking bureaucracy itself.

Secretive behavior may also, of course, hinder one's competitors, thereby giving rise to a variety of intelligence activities on the part of foreign policy bureaucracies. Although some (and unquestionably the most publicized) intelligence operations are covert, the bulk rely upon the analysis of more or less readily accessible information from foreign countries. In his chapter on "Public Perspectives in Closed Societies," Richard L. Merritt reviews some techniques that have been used to explore aspects of society and politics in the Soviet Union and other East European countries and suggests ways in which the findings could be made even more useful to scholars and policy analysts. Among these techniques are secondary analysis of sample surveys conducted in the countries themselves as well as interviews with refugees and short-term visitors to the West.

Two other chapters focus on participants in the foreign policy process. Charles F. Hermann outlines an answer to the question, "What Decision Units Shape Foreign Policy: Individual, Group, Bureaucracy?" By concentrating on situational variables and different stages of the policy process, he suggests what kinds of circumstances are likely to favor the priority of which decision units. Lawrence J. Korb, in his chapter on "The Military and Foreign Policy: The Role of the Joint Chiefs of Staff," discusses in greater detail the characteristics of one type of decision unit in the U.S. government. With their high degree of specialization and despite sometimes sharp interservice rivalries, the Chiefs have played a modifying but only rarely innovative role in the foreign policy process.

Foreign Policy Research and Policymaking

The material covered in this portion of the volume comprises a set of insights into the foreign policy process, not an elaborated or integrated framework encompassing all its aspects. Many are the variables to be considered; many, the research approaches that are appropriate. This is particularly true if we want a more generalized model of the foreign policy process rather than one describing the United States system alone. To complicate matters still more, changes over time must be accounted for. But here is not the place to discuss in detail all these needs for concepts, propositions, operationalizations, data, and integration of data and theory.

In one sense we can be quite optimistic about the future of foreign policy analysis. An immense amount of intellectual energy has been turned to exploring aspects of the process of foreign policymaking. It includes both microanalytic studies of how decisionmakers behave to macroanalytic mapping of patterns of interstate behavior. Moreover, syntheses that appear from time to time rely ever more on new insights and data derived from behavioral approaches. There is no good reason to assume that either of these trends will be stopped. Similarly, there is no good reason why we cannot expect in the not-too-distant future a thoroughly solid analysis of the foreign policy process that is grounded on empirically-based theory.

What is proceeding more slowly is the acceptance by the policymaking community of the methods, findings, and theories of behaviorally-oriented foreign policy analysts. A generation and more ago, foreign policy scholars and foreign policymaking personnel were highly interchangeable. Both shared an intellectual tradition at once historical and legalistic—one that viewed the international arena as one in which states mainly pursued power objectives in peace and war. Among the new orientations produced by scholarship since the 1930s are some that rely upon a high degree of methodological and statistical expertise, not easily acquired by the "generalist." Increasingly, in the field of foreign policy analysis, we have been moving in the direction of Sir Charles Snow's "two cultures."

Efforts to bridge the two cultures have not always been successful. It is one thing, for instance, to understand the parameters of public opinion, quite another to see their usefulness in foreign policymaking. Similarly, foreign policymakers may find fascinating studies that delineate patterns of interaction based on event data. They may nonetheless still be at a loss to see how such studies help them when, perhaps, a terrorist gang has occupied one of their overseas posts. To what extent can a foreign ministry actually use the files of data culled from *The New York Times* by scholars interested in developing empirically-based theory?

By posing such problems, I am suggesting neither that the intellectual gap is unbridgeable nor that policy analysts and policymakers have made no efforts to find common ground. To the contrary, numerous such efforts have made substantial progress. The point is rather that we still have a long distance to go. It may indeed turn out that the more pessimistic comments of some scholars are justified—that policymakers are interested only in data and theories that will support the position they intend to take anyway. But it is more likely in the long run that even the most opportunistic policymaker will find it imperative to take account of contradictory data and theories if they are solidly validated.

The other side of this particular coin is that scholars who rely overly much on the policymaking community for cues to the sorts of interests that they should pursue and the kinds of data they should collect can easily lose sight of their scientific objectives, such as the development of explanatory theory. The latter requires basic research the relevance of which to policy may not be immediately apparent. And it requires a willingness to go against prevailing orthodoxies, even if this means long years of research that finds no funding from foundations or governmental sources.

For all these reasons we can expect that the convergence of scholars and policymakers will never be complete. Nor should it be, if we want to keep our understanding of foreign relations open to new ideas and information, however uncomfortable they may be vis-à-vis current thinking and policy. What we can rather expect is the continued growth of the new profession of information brokers, who can translate present findings and theorizing into a language that the policymaking community can accept, and can indicate to scholars the sorts of things that would be useful knowing from the policymakers' point of view.

Policies for National Security

The foreign policy decision process produces a wide range of policies— some of them formulated hastily in situations of crises, others the result of long and serious bargaining among governmental agencies as well as nongovernmental actors, still others the consequences of oversight, default, or unintended and perhaps undesired side-effects of more carefully considered decisions. Such policies pertain to national security, the economic well-being of the country's citizens, exchanges of scholars and scientific information, adjustments of territorial disputes, and a host of other matters.

Part V of this volume focuses particularly upon national security policy. Ernst W. Gohlert examines "National Security Policy Formation in Comparative Perspective." Outlining ways to develop a "security index," he suggests some of its analytic uses as well as specific albeit tentative propositions which it can test.

Ralph Sanders, in his chapter on "Technology Transfer and Détente," and Rodney L. Huff, writing on "Nuclear Reactors and Foreign Policy: Challenges of a Global Technology," both analyze some implications for American policy of transfers of U.S. technology to other countries. Sanders looks at stances adopted by key policymakers, both individuals and groups, in recent debates about such transfers to the Soviet Union. Huff, considering the dangers of an uncontrolled spread of nuclear technologies, discusses means for guarding against abuse, both in a technical or specific sense and with respect to changes in the structure of the international system.

Finally, William H. Overholt and Marylin Chou examine the origin and uses of "Foreign Policy Doctrines," especially those such as the Monroe and Truman doctrines that defined U.S. national security conceptions, but also others, such as the "Open Door" policy in China. Although their use entails dangers, the authors argue, including potential ridigity and decreased responsiveness to changes in the international system, these doctrines can be extremely valuable for developing integrated policies and enlisting public support for them.

On the Sociology of Foreign Policy Studies

Taken in its entirety, this volume suggests both the possibilities and limited perspectives of foreign policy studies in the United States. On the one hand, work is proceeding in the immense task of turning the study of foreign policymaking from a journalistic art into a science that can develop and apply (at least preliminary) theory. Overall frameworks are increasingly explicit and systematic, not merely unintegrated and often self-contradictory views of the world of foreign policy. Data-based generalizations are replacing sweeping judgments based on anecdotal evidence and insight, often brilliant but sometimes also erratic. Deductive theory, even if rudimentary in form, is beginning to crowd out what was heretofore a mass of specifications that defied generalization and, ultimately, explanation. The papers presented in this volume suggest some of the directions in which foreign policy studies can move and are in fact moving.

The volume, on the other hand, also underlines persistent gaps in the field of foreign policy studies. Is this a consequence of the procedures used for selecting contributions? Quite possibly so, but I think not. Notices of the pending volume were sent to members of the Policy Studies Organization and other professional associations interested in international affairs; these notices outlined a rather broad and comparative approach to foreign policy analysis and requested submissions of ideas and abstracts of articles to be included in the volume. From among the many suggestions I selected the set of 27 that seemed to be both intrinsically interesting and related to each other, however vaguely. A review of the manuscripts submitted by this set of potential authors produced the 17 articles included here. The final selection, I feel, is representative of the theoretic concerns and approaches embodied in both the initial set of about five times that many suggestions as well as the field of foreign policy studies as a whole.

One notable gap, despite a couple of exceptions (here represented by the chapters by Appleton and Gohlert), is a blurring of any truly comparative perspective. The more we can learn about U.S. foreign policy, of course, the better off we are. And numerous scholars have paid serious attention elsewhere to the foreign policy processes of other countries.

More to the point in this regard is that few of those developing *systematic* theory about *processes* (as opposed to, e.g., correlates and outcomes, including "event" data) pay much heed to what happens in other countries. However well developed analyses of American foreign policy processes may be, the more general field of foreign policy decisionmaking, which is necessarily comparative and nonparochial, remains essentially inchoate, reliant upon anecdotal evidence, and neglected.

Second, students of foreign policy decisionmaking remain especially fascinated with national security. Again, this is as understandable, given the state of the world, as it is helpful for viewing the role of the United States in this world. The problem here is threefold: (1) since not all countries are as concerned with national security—nor do they have such world-wide responsibilities—as the United States, a scholarly emphasis on it militates against a more general, comparative study of the foreign policy process; (2) the stress accorded national security even in the United States means that other, increasingly critical areas of foreign policy, such as international financial policy, are slighted by precisely those who should be most concerned with them; (3) a strong emphasis in the scholarly literature on national security not only reflects but also in its own way justifies an overconcern with this topic on the part of U.S. policymakers. As Swift points out, it is also possible to view international interaction and foreign policy from the perspective of individual, human values.

A third area of concern is the continuing low level of meaningful exchange between foreign policy practitioners and academic experts. As suggested earlier, a generation of policy studies scholars using new methodologies and systematic approaches seems scarcely to have made a dent in the armor of entrenched bureaucrats dealing with foreign policy on a day-to-day basis. Whether the fault, if fault it be, lies with the abstruseness of the behavioral scientists or the obtuseness of policymaking officials is not at issue here. More to the point is that breakthroughs are needed more effectively to bridge the communication gap.

It bears restating that *with some notable exceptions* these laments—to put them in their strongest form: parochialism, obsession with national security, and irrelevance to the policymaking community—characterize the entire field of foreign policy studies. In all fairness, the individual items in this volume accomplish what they set out to do; and perhaps no single volume on so complex a topic can slay all the intellectual dragons that beset us. The field is in its infant stages in scientific terms. It is merely to be expected that American policy scientists should concentrate first of all on both what they know best and what the policymaking community itself sets out as its overriding concern. And, if the sociology of knowledge in other fields can serve as a guide, we may further expect rapid strides toward the development of empirically-based, general theory on policymaking in foreign affairs. The present volume points to some of the ways toward this goal.

Part I
Constraints from the
External Environment

2

Morality and Foreign Policy

Richard N. Swift

To talk about moral standards in international relations has, for some time now, been unfashionable.[a] After all, some political scientists argue, our business is not to weigh values. Indeed, many have attempted to create a "value-free" science by vainly trying to emulate natural scientists and economists in the mistaken belief that values do not enter into their work.[b]

But moral issues are inevitable in international relations,[c] and we owe it to ourselves to ask, especially since the Vietnam débacle, if the United States is properly prepared to face up to its moral responsibilities. For an answer, we may usefully look back to the time before scholars began debating the merits of mathematics and models, when the "great debate" between "realists" and "idealists" ensued (cf. Kennan, 1951, and Morgenthau, 1951; for rebuttal, Cook and Moos, 1954). One wonders today whether abandoning that debate in the forties and fifties was less a methodological decision than an easy way of avoiding difficult moral issues. Had we stayed then with the challenges posed, we might have been willing to formulate real alternatives to the notion of *national interest* and to ask whether that norm was in fact a banner to which the wise and honest could repair—that is, whether it sufficed to meet contemporary needs or whether it was an idea that had outlived its usefulness.

If one relates the national interest to fundamental democratic hypotheses, one recalls that the Declaration of Independence proclaims that governments are instituted among men to secure certain "unalienable rights," among which are not the national interest, but only the interests of individuals. Emphasizing the individual, as the Declaration does, is really the key to putting national interest in a democratic perspective. What has been missing from past discussions of national interest is an appreciation of the need to define *national interest* in terms of the interests of the *national*, the individual citizen, rather than of the *nation*, the institution. Morality does not require us to advance the national interest of all states at all times, or,

---

[a] Major exceptions are the publications of the Council on Religion and International Affairs, especially *Worldview*.

[b] Examples in fact abound of natural scientists who are fearful that some of their research puts humanity at risk and of economists concerned about the inadequacy of their theories in the face of simultaneous inflation and recession.

[c] See below for specific examples.

15

indeed, of any state at any time, if the state does not, as an institution, advance the superior interest of all of us as people. Contrary to Hans Morgenthau's dictum,[d] the national interest is not a function of true morality. The only true morality is individual morality, and to invest the national interest with true morality requires us to concern ourselves first with individuals—and not just our fellow nationals, either, but all individuals everywhere.

The moral component in national issues was long ago pointed to by Arnold Wolfers (1952, pp. 500-01):

Decision makers are faced with the moral problem . . . of choosing first the values which deserve protection, with national independence ranking high not merely for its own sake but for the guarantee it may offer to values like liberty, justice and peace. . . . Policies of national security, far from being all good or all evil, may be morally praiseworthy or condemnable depending on their specific character and the particular circumstances of the case.

Wolfers elaborated his point by reminding us how pacifists opt out of communities when they decide not to go to war to preserve their states. And Wolfers' words later found living proof in the lives of Americans who made their way to Canada or Sweden to escape service in a Vietnam war of which they disapproved, even though it was being fought in the name of national security and interest.

These dissenters from the then existing order claimed that the alleged national interest was not their own; that merely to label something *national interest* did not imbue it with sanctity. They were reminding us all that they were not interested in an abstract United States, but in a United States that stood for something worth believing in. They were implicitly modifying Wolfers' statement by asserting that national independence ranked high as a value *only* if it offered to the individual guarantees of liberty, justice, and peace. Logically, national existence might have to come first, even as life must logically precede liberty and the pursuit of happiness, but men must still continue to judge states by human values because only human beings create either states or values. States have no independent volition, and democratic theory, at least, requires states to reflect human, individual values.

To judge the actions of the state by individual standards, however, requires one to concede the ultimate right, which Thomas Jefferson (1804) himself acknowledged, to jettison the state entirely if it fails to show any likelihood of fulfilling moral principles. It is in failing to concede this final possibility that the national interest standard fails completely; by concen-

---

[d] "It is not only a political necessity but also a moral duty for a nation to follow in its dealings with other nations but one guiding star, one standard for thought, one rule of action: The National Interest" (Morgenthau, 1951, p. 242).

trating on the nation and not on the individual, in fact, it almost forecloses the possibility of transcending itself.[e] Again, democratic theory requires a system to provide for change when it ceases to meet constitutionally established criteria; otherwise it cannot in perpetuity fulfill the individual's interests.

If we concentrate on national, rather than human interest, we almost automatically think first of state security. But as soon as we think in individual terms, we realize that to preserve a democratic United States, we must aim at enhancing the quality and quantity of individual freedom, at reducing the amounts spent unproductively on armaments, at increasing the percentages of funds disbursed to improve the quality of human life, at searching out with friends common solutions to common problems, and at reducing world tensions.

Thinking in terms of the individual, moreover, joins foreign and domestic concerns because, in order to enhance the extent and quality of freedom, we cannot help but worry about the impact of foreign policy upon civil liberties or think about the priorities we should assign to defense as opposed to public housing, urban renewal, and the environment. It becomes quite natural to incorporate into our decisionmaking the moral qualms about the treatment of Soviet Jews in relation to U.S. trade policy, the consequences for freedom of the U.S. policy on the UN embargo on South Africa and Rhodesia, the costs to mankind of nuclear tests, the importance to everyone of the "common heritage of mankind" in the oceans, and the implications of the contrast between standards of living in the United States and in less well-endowed states.

Concentrating on individual, human values would make us all more critical of foreign policy decisions. We could more easily insist that statesmen stop squandering funds—*our* tax money—on futile races for arms supremacy, and instead try harder to agree to regulate arms; that states enlarge UN peace-keeping capabilities; that they share more fully the costs of exploring space and preserving the environment. We would have a firmer base from which to insist on using the funds saved for undertakings important to democracy, like building houses and schools, improving medical care, making efficient use of the world's talents and resources, and vigorously searching for political substitutes for military security.

A quest for better standards of living and larger individual freedom would turn statesmen more toward international law and organization as instruments for achieving their goals. They would have to concentrate less on national and more on international institutions, standards, and interests.

---

[e] Morgenthau (1952) himself visualized a future "when the national state will have been replaced by another mode of organization," but he writes of the "usurpation of the national interest" by other interests, as though the process were not legitimate.

They would pay more attention to the UN, whose members are an incipient community and whose Purposes and Principles represent a consensus. They would use the UN, when it was the best available instrument, not for advancing national interests alone but for advancing the interests of all mankind. Developing means of cooperating with friends through the UN, the European Community, through multilateral aid programs, would take on new significance, and regulating armaments would automatically become more important than developing them. When improving the quality of life and freedom rather than merely maintaining national interest becomes a primary goal, settling major differences with one's principal antagonists receives a higher priority because resolving disputes helps free mankind from overwhelming arms burdens. Had decisionmakers applied this conception of interest earlier, the United States, for instance, might, long before the era of détente, have considered establishing mutually beneficial relations with the U.S.S.R., the People's Republic of China, Cuba, and North Vietnam.

To substitute the interests of individuals for the interests of states as a standard for conducting foreign policy is not to usher in the millennium. It certainly is not an automatic process, nor does it mean suspending personal judgment. Far from it, it means holding members of international institutions accountable to international law and to the charters and other international treaties to which they have suscribed. But it also means participating constructively in the work of international organizations, attempting to develop international institutions, and, above all, recognizing that reconciling one's own moral claims with those of others is a fundamental and legitimate requirement of international democracy.[f]

Applying moral standards internationally is even more complex than it is domestically. But in facing the difficulties, one need not mask the moral dilemmas. One should try to distinguish honestly between morality, which has to do with virtue and rightness, and *raison d'état* disguised as morality, and one should condemn decisionmakers who misuse moral arguments for selfish purposes or who justify tactics by irrelevant and self-serving "moralism." One should not automatically accept national interest as a moral standard or err, as John Foster Dulles so often did, in confusing expediency and morality (Hoopes, 1973). If a state acts expediently, a statesman should admit it. By being frank, he tries to save himself and his countrymen from *hubris*: Americans, for instance, would never have been led to assume that a *Pax Americana* or an American Century were moral imperatives. We would instead have acknowledged the moral imperfections in our own policies, pointed them out in the policies of others, and tried, in all cases, to work toward an improved international environment.

---

[f]Northrop (1952) makes such an attempt, but it is not entirely satisfactory.

Facing moral problems honestly helps clarify one's thinking and makes one's behavior more rational—two great assets in conducting foreign policy.

"Realists" will say that these transformations in values and approaches are impossible, but realists always find it impossible to do what ultimately proves inevitable. The existing order has always seemed quite immutable to them—and probably never more so than just before the deluge. It is no doubt difficult in some quarters to think of substituting an individual, human, moral standard for a national one. Changes in all traditional ways of carrying on public or private business are well nigh impossible in the minds of those concerned only with the past.

On the other hand, if it is apparent to us that our norms, as well as our times, are out of joint, we ought freely to admit the fact, to say openly that we need a new standard, and to welcome a standard that is no longer merely national, but international. Political compromises will be inevitable. But we ought not to mistake the real for the ideal. We should set our sights on goals that transcend reality and move toward an ideal, instead of walking blindly, as we started to do in Vietnam, into a sea of certain destruction.

References

Cook, Thomas I. and Malcolm Moos. 1954. *Power through Purpose: The Realism of Idealism as a Basis for Foreign Policy*. Baltimore: Johns Hopkins University Press.

Hoopes, Townsend. 1973. *The Devil and John Foster Dulles*. Boston: Little, Brown.

Jefferson, Thomas. 1804. Letter to Judge Tyler.

Kennan, George F. 1951. *American Diplomacy, 1900-1950*. Chicago: University of Chicago Press.

Morgenthau, Hans J. 1952. "Another 'Great Debate': The National Interest of the United States." *American Political Science Review* 46:4 (December): 961-88.

———. 1951. *In Defense of National Interest*. New York: Knopf.

Northrop, F.S.C. 1952. *The Taming of the Nations: A Study of the Cultural Bases of International Policy*. New York: Macmillan.

Wolfers, Arnold. 1952. "'National Security' as an Ambiguous Symbol." *Political Science Quarterly* 67:4 (December): 481-502.

3

Foreign Policy Outputs and International Law

Don C. Piper

In examining the complexities of foreign policy decisionmaking and actions, it is frequently very difficult for an observer to assess with precision the importance or relevance of a particular variable in the decisionmaking process. This is especially the case when one attempts to evaluate the influence and relevance of international law rules in the decisionmaking process. In simple terms, our conventional wisdom sometimes suggests that states (i.e., decisionmakers) in adopting a course of action either adhere to or ignore the rules of international law. It is usually asserted that on matters of little consequence the decisionmaker acts consistently with the existing rules of international law but that on matters that threaten to impair the national security, the decisionmaker follows a course of action based upon more important "political" rather than legal considerations.

Upon examination this simple dichotomy of adherence or neglect does not reflect accurately the influence of the international legal order upon the decisionmaker and the reciprocal influence of the decisionmaker upon the international legal order. The relationship or fit between international law and foreign policy actions is a subtle and flexible one. It is also, as indicated above, a reciprocal relationship whereby the decisionmaker is influenced by the legal order and in turn may influence the legal order in a way that facilitates the growth of the legal order. In addressing this relationship, I propose first to summarize briefly the nature of the international legal system. Then I shall consider the possible relationships between the decisionmaker's actions and the rules of international law.

Since World War II, the international legal order has undergone substantial growth and development, especially in terms of the types of state activities that are now regulated by rules of international law. The growth of the law has been particularly evident in the proliferation of general multilateral, lawmaking treaties. While this growth is important, some lacunae persist in the legal order, especially in matters relating to the use of armed force and the regulation of recent technological developments. In addition, the international legal order remains a primitive legal system. This is the case at least to the extent that there is no institutional arrangement for regularized and systematic lawmaking to change the law and to keep it current with the political, economic, social, and technological changes in the international community.

21

Many of the rules of international law, especially particular treaty rules, may be stated with precision, and disputes regarding the rules may be readily arbitrated or adjudicated. Other rules, and this is also especially the case with regard to rules relating to the use of armed force, lack precision and are less susceptible of definitive interpretation by either an international legal or political organ.

The international legal system is also a horizontal rather than a vertical legal system in the sense that there does not exist an institutional arrangement that provides for the mandatory interpretation and application of the rules of law that are in dispute between states. Accordingly, states (i.e., decisionmakers) may enjoy a relatively wide latitude in interpreting and applying the rules of international law in specific courses of action.

As a consequence of the legal system, a decisionmaker will confront many courses of action wherein the international legal rules are precisely stated and provide specific behavioral guidance. In other situations, however, the decisionmaker may contemplate a proposed course of action wherein the existing rules of international law lack precision and definitive guidance. Where this is the case the decisionmaker remains under the influence of the international legal order but enjoys a greater opportunity to influence that order (cf. Chayes, 1974, pp. 26-27, 86-87).

In evaluating the actions of a decisionmaker and his observance of international law, I utilize two assumptions that should be stated. First, I believe that a decisionmaker extends the highest priority to the maintenance of national security and the promotion of the national interest, however he may define it. Second, I assume that in any course of action, a decisionmaker wishes to remain within the boundaries of the international legal order. To put the assumption differently, I assume that no decisionmaker wishes to reject openly and publicly the international legal order and adopt a course of action that is clearly prohibited by the legal order.

It is also important to understand that the decisionmaker's perception of the international event influences his choice of the applicable legal rules. For example, those who perceived the conflict in Vietnam to be an international conflict accompanied by aggression from North Vietnam invoked a series of legal rules based upon the right of self-defense and the illegality of aggression. In contrast, those who perceived the conflict as an instance of civil strife between two contending political elites for the control of a single state invoked a series of legal rules reflecting noninvolvement by third parties in civil strife (for differing views, cf. U.S. Department of State, 1966; Falk, 1966). Here, as in other foreign policy events, the decisionmaker's perception of the event leads to the invocation of the appropriate legal rules.

Accordingly as a decisionmaker contemplates a proposed course of action he may receive differing, and possibly conflicting, recommendations of the governing legal rules because his advisers hold differing perceptions of the event and its importance. In addition, his advisers representing differing bureaus, agencies, and departments may offer differing legal advice based upon their bureaucratic orientations.[a]

As a decisionmaker considers and evaluates proposed courses of action, I suggest that one or the other of the following propositions is likely to be the relationship between the course of action and the rules of international law.

Proposition I: The decisionmaker will adhere to the existing rules of international law in a course of action so long as he believes that he can do so without impairing the national security.

Proposition II: If the decisionmaker perceives that his adherence to the existing rules of international law in a course of action will impair the national security or that the existing rules are inadequate or incomplete for a course of action, then he will assert a new interpretation of the existing rules or assert a new rule of international law.

Although I shall concentrate my attention on Proposition II, Proposition I deserves brief attention. Persuasive evidence in support of this proposition is the magnitude of regularized, continuing, nonconflictual intercourse between the states in the international community.[b] Decisionmakers understand that close adherence to the existing rules of international law provides for the predictable and regularized behavior that is essential for a minimum international community. The benefits derived from maintaining predictable behavior, even at some cost to national policy, and avoiding international surprises is perhaps the most persuasive element in facilitating adherence to the rules of international law. Some might also suggest that the decisionmaker accepts the existing rules of international law because they cover matters of little consequence and their utilization can be accomplished with little or no cost to the state. Although the evidence may support a conclusion that adherence to many of the existing rules of international law can be accomplished with little cost to the state, I am convinced that the evidence does not support the assertion that these rules always pertain to matters of little consequence.

Because of the nature of the international legal system discussed above,

---

[a] See Chayes (1974, pp. 19-23) for examples of the differing legal advice regarding the appropriate American response to the Cuban missile crisis.

[b] Richard Falk (1968, p. 74) points out that adherence to the rules of international law is facilitated and promoted by the "rule orientation" of the members of the bureaucracy who have responsibility for most noncrisis foreign policy actions.

a decisionmaker when confronted with the evidence that adherence to the existing rules of international law may impair the national security or that the existing rules are inadequate or inappropriate has the opportunity to set forth a unilateral interpretation of existing rules or the assertion of a new rule of law—that is, the decisionmaker will assert the right of the state to undertake certain specified action, which until that time had not been legally recognized, with the action being permissible within the general principles of international law.

As examples of the unilateral assertion of a new rule of international law or the interpretation of an existing rule, I offer the following illustrations.[c]

First, the United States "quarantine" to prevent the introduction of offensive missiles into Cuba in 1962: The "quarantine" was an assertion of a new right (i.e., rule of law) that a state with the endorsement of a regional organization could interdict ships on the high seas to prevent the introduction of offensive weapons into a designated area.

Second, the proclamation by President Truman in 1945 of the "Policy of the United States with Respect to the Natural Resources of the Subsoil and Sea Bed of the Continental Shelf" (Whiteman, 1965, iv, pp. 756-57): In this proclamation the president asserted a rule regarding the continental shelf—that a state could place under its jurisdiction and control for purposes of utilization and conservation the natural resources on the sea bed and subsoil of its adjacent continental shelf. In this instance, technological developments, especially off-shore oil drilling, dictated a new rule regarding rights of jurisdiction. In asserting the new rule, the United States did not upset the existing rules by expanding the territorial sea or asserting rights of sovereignty over fishing or navigation activities in the waters superjacent to the continental shelf.

Third, the Canadian government establishment in 1970 of an Arctic Pollution Control Zone of 100 miles above the 60th parallel in which the Canadian government will exercise rights of jurisdiction regarding navigation, construction, and operation of vessels including the right to prohibit free navigation (Canada, 1970): The purpose of such a control zone is to enable the Canadian government to exercise jurisdiction over all shipping activities that could potentially lead to oil spills that could damage the Arctic tundra. Thus, it is asserted that a state has a right to exercise limited rights of jurisdiction over portions of the high seas adjacent to its coast in order to protect the environmental balance along its coast.

Fourth, the extension in 1972 by the government of Iceland of an exclusive fishing zone from 12 miles to 50 miles from baselines around the

---

[c] The illustrations offered here relate to unilateral action by a single state. It is equally likely that a small number of states will act together in "unilaterally" asserting a rule of law against other members of the international community. For example, in 1952, Chile, Ecuador, and Peru signed the Declaration of Santiago on the Maritime Zone in which they asserted national control over a 200-mile territorial sea adjacent to their coasts for the purpose of conservation and development of the marine life found in the zone (Whiteman, 1965, IV, pp. 1089-90).

Icelandic coast: This unilateral extension was invoked against the United Kingdom and justified on the ground that exclusive fishing rights were essential for Iceland's economic survival and to conserve the fishing areas. It also involved the unilateral termination of a 1961 agreement with the United Kingdom that permitted fishing outside of a 12-mile limit.

There is no doubt that this opportunity to assert a new rule of law may be abused by a decisionmaker who may deliberately or inadvertently pursue an illegal course of action and try to cover it with a legal explanation. Indeed, readers may suggest instances in which they believe that this has occurred. Although such occurrences may not be prevented or stopped, they do not receive community approval and the support that is necessary for the acceptance of a customary rule of international law.

Unless a decisionmaker is prepared to act openly in contempt of the international legal order, there are two factors that serve as restraints on his freedom of action to assert new rules of law or new interpretations of existing rules. These restraints serve to influence the decisionmakers to act within rather than outside the legal order.

To assert that a decisionmaker is influenced to act within the framework of the international legal order is not to assert that a decisionmaker ignores political or policy considerations. It is rather to assert that the decisionmaker examines these considerations within the context of their relationship with the legal order.

One important restraint is the prospect of general approval or disapproval by other members of the international community. Notwithstanding the ambiguity and lacunae in the law, rules of international law do exist. Other decisionmakers acknowledge these lawful rules and operate with a presumption that the behavior they regulate will occur within specified, predictable boundaries. Accordingly, a decisionmaker must secure support for his action while at the same time preserving the general community belief in and support for lawful, regularized, and predictable patterns of behavior.

Not all of the assertions of a new rule or interpretation of existing rules will be accepted by other states. Indeed the United States has protested the Canadian action in establishing the control zone on the ground that such action should only be undertaken after consultation and negotiation. Expressions of disagreement may vary from verbal protests, to the filing of legal action before the International Court of Justice, as was done by the United Kingdom against Iceland, or the initiation of complaints before the U.N. Security Council.[d] It is not inconceivable that in the face of strong protests a state might amend or reverse its course of action. The unilateral

---

[d] In 1972 the United Kingdom filed suit against Iceland in the International Court of Justice, asserting that Iceland could not invoke the 50-mile rule against the United Kingdom. In 1974 the court held that the new fishing zone could not be invoked against the United Kingdom and that Iceland was not in law able unilaterally to exclude the United Kingdom from the fishing zone that had been agreed to in 1961 (International Court of Justice, 1975).

assertion of a rule of law is not in itself sufficient to provide a legal status. That legal status comes from the approval or in some instances the absence of disapproval of the other states in the international community.

An incremental change in the content of the law is more likely to be accepted by other states than a radical or unpredictable change that may be perceived as destabilizing or conferring an undue advantage on a particular state. Thus, the Cuban "quarantine" had to fit within the existing rules of free navigation as well as those relating to naval blockades and the use of armed force.[e] The continental shelf proclamation and the Canadian pollution control zone had to fit within the existing rules of a limited territorial sea and the rights of free navigation. Maintenance of the rights of ocean fishing was also important in the former case. The Icelandic action was not accepted by the International Court of Justice in part because the government sought unilaterally to terminate a previous agreement with the United Kingdom. Consequently the action did not "fit" within the existing rules.

Another restraint that should be noted is the realization by the decisionmaker that the new rule represents a legal precedent that may be employed in the future by other states.[f] Once President Truman issued the U.S. continental shelf proclamation, the United States could not deny to other states a right to announce a similar doctrine to the possible disadvantage of some United States interests. In a like manner, the Canadian government must permit the United States or other states to initiate similar pollution control zones even to the disadvantage of some Canadian interests.

This ability of a decisionmaker to assert a new rule and thus contribute to the growth of the international legal order is important and significant in view of the absence of any regularized procedures in the community to change the law and introduce new rules of law. The process outlined above may be one of the ways in which the currency of the law may be maintained. The full community may benefit from and readily endorse unilateral assertions that generate new legal relationships and rights. This process appears to be wholly compatible with the existence of a customary international legal order.

If the process is abused by a decisionmaker, the process is dysfunctional for the international community. The process will be eufunctional for the community when constructive rules are the result of unilateral action.

---

[e] Theodore Sorensen (1965, p. 706) reports that Llewellyn Thompson stressed the importance of legal justification of the United States action in the missile crisis. Legal arguments were apparently considered to be influential on the "legalistic-minded decisionmakers in the Kremlin."

[f] Harlan Cleveland (1963, p. 647) declares that concern for precedent is one of the five lessons of crisis diplomacy. "Watch carefully the precedents you set. You will have to live with the institutions you create. The law you make may be your own."

It would appear that the international community benefited from the United States continental shelf proclamation. The utility of the new rule was obvious to many states that quickly issued similar rules. The doctrine was subsequently incorporated into treaty law in the 1958 Geneva Convention on the Continental Shelf. (It is probably too soon to determine definitively whether the community benefited in a legal sense from the quarantine or pollution control zone.)

As I indicated at the start, it is very difficult for an observer to assess precisely how the rules of international law enter into the decisionmaking process. We can, however, evaluate the relationship between the rules of international law and foreign policy outputs. In doing so, we need to go beyond the simple dichotomy of adherence or rejection and examine the relationship in terms of its potential to maintain and support the international legal order or perhaps to facilitate the growth of the legal order. A variety of foreign policy outputs needs to be examined to ascertain if the propositions suggested above can be supported.

References

Canada. 1970. Arctic Waters Pollution Prevention Act. Canada, R.S.C., 1st supp., c. 2.

Chayes, Abram. 1974. *The Cuban Missile Crisis*. New York: Oxford University Press.

Cleveland, Harlan. 1963. "Crisis Diplomacy." *Foreign Affairs* 41:4 (July):638-49.

Falk, Richard A. 1966. "International Law and the United States Role in the Viet Nam War." *Yale Law Journal* 75:7 (June):1122-60.

_____. 1968. *Legal Order in a Violent World*. Princeton, N.J.: Princeton University Press.

International Court of Justice. 1975. "Fisheries Jurisdiction Case (United Kingdom, v. Iceland)." *American Journal of International Law* 69:1 (January):154-74.

Sorensen, Theodore. 1965. *Kennedy*. New York: Harper and Row.

U.S. Department of State. 1966. "The Legality of United States Participation in the Defense of Viet-Nam" (Memorandum of 4 March 1966). Department of State Bulletin 54:1396 (28 March):474-89.

Whiteman, Marjorie M. 1965. *Digest of International Law*, 15 Volumes. Washington: Government Printing Office.

4

"You Can't Get There From Here"

*Aline O. Quester and
George H. Quester*

Are Americans too incremental and too optimistic in their political attitudes? The charge has often been made that this is particularly a problem for the execution of foreign policy. An attempt will be made here to trace such tendencies to concepts Americans may borrow from the free exchange of the economic market place.

If Americans distrust the market economy for macroeconomic considerations, we may yet have a high trust for it on microeconomic questions—perhaps too high an instinctive trust. In everyday life, we broadly assume that one can get more if he is ready to pay more and that one can sell more if he is ready to lower his price. If commodity shortages threaten, raising the price should take care of the problem. If some kinds of labor are in short supply, let the market handle it. If unemployment threatens (except for Keynesian-model unemployment induced by shortages of aggregate demand), labor is presumably just overpriced.

Microeconomics has already done a fuller analysis of some exceptions to the rule. Such "cheap goods" as hamburger may sell less if they drop in price, because they thereby increase the consumer's real income enough to allow him to buy steak instead of hamburger once a week. "Backward bending supply curves" of various goods can be traced out, perhaps because the more highly paid laborer elects to take longer vacations or to refuse to work overtime. Yet the leap from rigorous economic analysis to common sense intuition is not always completed. It will be argued here that, especially in foreign policy areas, the phenomenon of market anomaly is more widespread than normally assumed, that it relates very importantly to the politics of force and violence and coercion, and that it may play a much more oppressive role in the future.

Americans have recently had several interesting brushes with unresponsive market mechanisms that are related in each case somewhat to the perversities of the outside world. One example appears with efforts to raise a volunteer army to fight or deter future wars. An interesting coalition of left-of-center antimilitarists and rightwing laissez-faire economists has evinced great enthusiasm for the prospect that the draft can be permanently eliminated—that one can get enough ordinary soldiers and military physicians if the wage is only raised high enough (Miller, 1968). But would this indeed be true in the event of another shooting war? It may well be that

29

not enough men could now be recruited no matter how high the pay and indeed that the maximum of supply would be less than the minimum needed as the supply curve bent backwards (see Figure 4-1). The more military physicians or ordinary soldiers are paid for their first hitch, the more money they would put in the bank and the fewer of them would choose to reenlist for a second hitch. Current enlistment terms typically run three or four years. Do we have to make the term twenty years in order to ensure that we do not lose more soldiers than we gain by raising military pay? If we did, of course, we would only be replacing "slavery" with "indentured servitude," not quite the great leap to a free market economy.

A parallel example most recently capturing American attention appears in Arab attitudes—most especially the attitudes of Saudi Arabia—toward oil production. Would the Arabs sell more oil if the price were decreased? Probably not. Will they sell more oil if the price is increased? Also very probably not, since the surplus of revenue collected indeed may put the supplier in the mood to decrease his production either for fear of accumulating too many cash reserves and/or losing too many oil reserves or even possibly for the reason of simple indifference to any further increases in national income. If the outside world desires to consume 100 units of petroleum in 1980, then there may be no price at which the suppliers will be willing to produce more than 90 (Akins, 1973).

A traditional analyst of power politics might have suggested that coercion always becomes necessary sooner or later, when "free exchange" reaches its upper limit on the goods and services that will be voluntarily delivered. Perhaps the forcible "opening of Japan" to trade in the nineteenth century supplies the model, or the Opium War, when Britain found the Chinese too disinterested in foreign exchange to be willing to sell more tea.

But Americans have had only a passing acquaintance with the total inelasticity issue in their domestic economic life, and it has not been central to their experience. For a most atypical example, the classic rationalization for slavery in the American South followed strikingly similar lines. No one, it was argued, would on a voluntary basis be willing to do the hard field work required for the Southern economy; if the pay went up to attract the required force, workers would divert their extra pay to cutting their work week to three days, etc.(Ruffin, 1973).

One must, of course, be more than a little wary of all such rationalizations for coercion. What is explained as necessary to recruit the necessary quantity of labor might simply be a cover for paying less for the labor, when the necessary quantity would indeed have showed up under voluntary circumstances. Perhaps a volunteer army can be recruited, if we only pay enough; in such a case, the draft has only been a particularly vicious tax, supporting national defense by cutting the personal income of the very

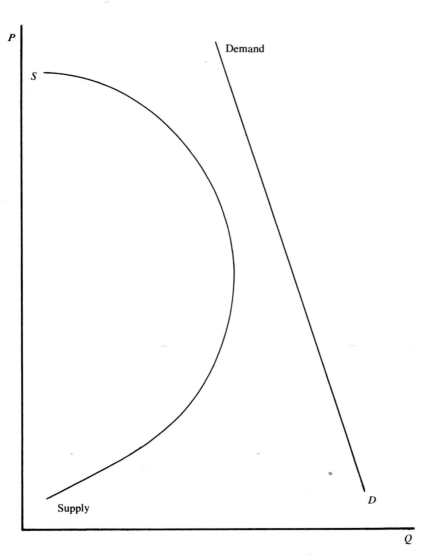

Figure 4-1. Backward Bending Supply Curve

persons who have to do the fighting. And so with Southern slavery, which may only have been exploitative, and never "necessary."

Yet although this kind of "unresponsive market" reasoning is sometimes misapplied as a cover for simple greed, we may have been rejecting it overly much in our everyday American approach to policy, especially when it relates to the foreign policy problems posed by the underdeveloped world. Americans are often labeled as being too pragmatic here. Perhaps the problem is rather that some aspects of the world's problems are *per se* resistant to pragmatism. Perhaps sufficient foreign oil will not be forthcoming, even when Southern labor was.

Other kinds of market anomaly can also plague foreign policy, particularly an American foreign policy dedicated to preventing violent revolution and fostering economic and political development. The obverse of the argument for slavery applies to a form of unemployment basically unrelated to Keynesian models but perhaps closely tied to Marx's predictions (Robinson, 1951). Unfortunately for Marx, the predictions are typically not yet confirmable for any industrialized society—the very ones he focused on. They may nonetheless have great application to underdeveloped countries plagued with "overpopulation" and/or "underemployment." This form of unemployment model basically argues that capital-intensive methods will be far superior to labor-intensive methods for producing whatever is needed (in particular, for what is most needed where there is overpopulation—food). As long as large inputs of capital are not available, however, large quantities of labor will not have appropriate amounts of capital to be paired off with. Such labor might be kept "employed," but only in less efficient "labor-intensive" ways. Indeed, at some point, the true marginal product of such labor might become negative, as labor basically simply stands in the way of a productive capital-using approach (Grant, 1971).

Consider a field that once produced 100 units of wheat with 100 laborers working all over it. With a modern tractor, one might produce 200 units, but only if the labor force is reduced to 40, so that the surplus 60 do not get in the tractor's way. This situation would thus amount to yet another failure of market mechanisms to produce any equilibrium of supply and demand. If the supply of labor on hand were to be fully employed, the marginal product and wage would have to be negative. Workers will, of course, not offer themselves for a negative wage, but at the first noticeable positive wage, too many will come forward, as the supply curve of labor at this point is almost totally elastic (see Figure 4-2). When labor is needed, but will not come forward, we have noted that coercion typically follows. But what happens, when labor comes forward but is not needed? Coercion also results, but in a form, which in itself may cause many more policy worries, often called "revolution."

If an inability of the market to reconcile supply and demand becomes more typical, violence and/or the threat of violence may become more typical. Domestically, such threats of violence are regularized under the rubric of "law and order," of "taxes" and "regulation." In the foreign policy of international relations, however, it never becomes quite so regularized, as we talk more often of "war" and "revolution." As noted, we must anticipate being frustrated in the processes of free market exchange; we must also brace ourselves for the reactions when others are frustrated.

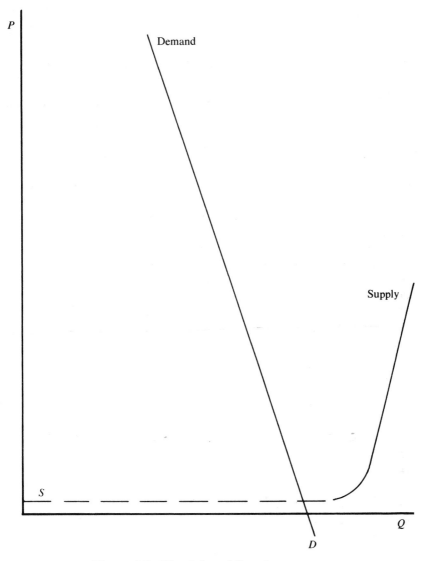

Figure 4-2. Elasticity of Supply

Attitudes toward American foreign policy are often sorted on a spectrum of liberal versus conservative, although any correlation here between domestic policy outlooks and willingness to intervene abroad often breaks down. After 1945, the "great debate" instead was often characterized as "idealist" versus "realist," the latter group presumably being more willing to use immoral means, indeed violent means, for possibly moral ends in the anarchic international arena. Yet, as exemplified best in the writings of

Hans Morgenthau, the "realist" pessimism hinged mostly on the anarchy of the international system in the absence of law and order and on the very possibly tautological argument that states would have to pursue power as the means to remaining states, as the means to achieving anything else.

The different kind of distinction that has been proposed here might lamentably sometimes have pessimistic implications for the domestic sphere as well as the international. All too often, "you can't get there from here." And too often, what worked to achieve good results up to this point cannot produce such results anymore since additional inputs would now begin to produce counterproductive outputs—that is, negative returns instead of just diminishing returns. This is profoundly antipragmatic, and antiincremental, and antioptimistic. It suggests periodic occasions for enormous "changes in the rules," whereby forced exchange will replace free exchange in what one side might style violence and another might call a revolution.

We are more used to switching back and forth from voluntary exchange to coercion in domestic society as the free market and the income tax somehow exist side by side. Yet, we may be systematically misremembering this mix of methods used at home and kidding ourselves that free exchange always can work. As suggested above, this can turn out to be most baffling and frustrating for our ventures into the international arena. Violence against us may catch us by surprise, as revolutionary wars occur where we had expected a "gradual process of economic development." We may also feel tempted to initiate violence ourselves, to our surprise, in places where we would have counted upon "free trade" to give us what we need.

References

Akins, James E. 1973. "The Oil Crisis: This Time the Wolf Is Here." *Foreign Affairs* 51:3 (April):462-90.

Grant, James P. 1971. "Marginal Men: The Global Unemployment Crisis." *Foreign Affairs* 50:1 (October):112-24.

Miller, James C., ed. 1968. *Why the Draft? The Case for a Volunteer Army.* Baltimore: Penguin.

Robinson, Joan. 1951. "Marx and Keynes," pp. 133-45, in *Collected Economic Papers.* Oxford: Basil Blackwell.

Ruffin, Edmund. 1963 (orig. 1853). "The Political Economy of Slavery," pp. 69-85, in Eric L. McKitrick, ed. *Slavery Defended: The Views of the Old South.* Englewood Cliffs, N.J.: Prentice-Hall.

**Part II
Domestic Constraints**

5

The Parochial Constraint on Foreign Policymaking

*Barry S. Rundquist and
David E. Griffith*

A long-debated question regarding the domestic sources of foreign policy is whether foreign policymaking is organized to accord disproportionate influence to those sectors of society that have the most to gain from military spending. If a government's foreign policymaking is so organized, it can be argued that *ceteris paribus* that government will be constrained to spend more for defense and to behave more aggressively in the international system than if its foreign policymaking is not so organized.

This "parochial constraint" hypothesis has proved remarkably resistant to verification. This indicates either that the hypothesis is invalid or that researchers have failed to ask the appropriate empirical questions about it. In this chapter, we break the concept of parochial constraint into two operational forms. We suggest that this splitting of the concept raises an appropriate empirical question and some interesting, albeit tentative, answers.

The Dynamic and Static Forms of the Parochial Constraint

Our distinction follows from the question: What is it that a sector can gain from military spending that, in the absence of intervening considerations, would constrain a policymaker from that sector to favor aggressive foreign policies? In other words, why would the parochial constraint constrain? We perceive two answers to this question. The first is that a policymaker, Actor A, would be constrained if his sector received more of whatever foreign policy benefits (e.g., military procurement expenditures) were available in a given period than did other sectors,[a] Why would this constrain Actor A to favor more aggressive foreign policies? Apparently because another actor with control over foreign policy benefits would trade some of those benefits to Actor A's sector for his support for aggressive foreign policies. For example, concerning American military programs, an argument has been made that the military services offer expenditure benefits

---

[a] We speak here of "sectors" in an effort to make our distinction as general as possible. The examples we use concern geographic areas, but in principle there is nothing that would prohibit the treatment of nongeographic "sectors" in the United States or other political systems.

to military committee members from defense-involved constituencies in return for committee approval of their program and budget requests (Niskanen, 1971). Such a trade may be explicit or anticipated, but without it there would seem to be no logical link between those sectors that receive more military expenditures than other sectors and aggressive foreign policies. Because it requires that some sectors receive more foreign policy benefits than other sectors at one point in time, we will term this the *static* form of the parochial constraint.

A second form, the *dynamic* form, is that policymakers would be constrained to favor more aggressive foreign policies if their sectors benefited directly from more aggressive foreign policies. The constraint would be direct if more aggressive foreign policies (e.g., wars or arms races) are associated with higher levels of military expenditures and a policymaker's sector received a proportionate or larger share of the increases in the overall level of expenditures. In this case, it is not a matter of some sectors getting more expenditure benefits than other sectors in a given period, but of a sector benefiting more when a foreign policy is more aggressive than when it is less aggressive. By benefit, we mean a real increase in a sector's economic well-being—that is, the wealth, employment, or some other economic value that military expenditures add to a sector minus what they detract from a sector. For example, if military employment can only be increased when civilian employment is decreased, the real benefit of such an increase would be negligible. Moreover, this second form of parochial constraint does not require that trading occur. Policymakers from defense-involved sectors need only know that their sectors benefit from aggressive foreign policies—even if for purely economic reasons (e.g., rifles are manufactured in their district).

It is useful to compare these two notions of the parochial constraint with Huntington's (1961) distinction between structural and strategic foreign policies. Strategic foreign policies, in his view, are those that concern the use of force in the international system; structural foreign policies are those that concern the distribution of resources within a country. This distinction essentially defines away the question of parochial constraints on strategic foreign policies. It assumes that parochially oriented actors are only interested in getting more of whatever foreign policy resources there are to get—that they are oblivious to strategic considerations. Similarly, it assumes that actors concerned with strategic policies care little about the domestic distribution of foreign policy resources. Our two forms of the parochial constraint suggest ways in which strategic and structural foreign policies are linked.

Relevant Research Findings

Given these two forms of the parochial constraint, a major empirical question is: Which cell in Table 5-1 characterizes the way in which a nation's foreign policymaking is organized? A partial answer to this question is suggested by the empirical studies of congressional military committees in the United States. These studies have examined the representation of defense-involved areas (i.e., districts, states) on the military committees as it relates to the static form of parochial constraint. For the most part, the findings of these studies have been negative. Areas represented on the military committees do not evidence more military contract dollars than areas not represented on these committees (Goss, 1972; Rundquist and Ferejohn, 1975). This suggests that the military committees are not characterized by the static form of the parochial constraint and therefore fit one of the two cells in the bottom row of Table 5-1.

Unfortunately, there has been no research on the dynamic form of parochial constraint. In an effort to establish whether or not the military committees would be subject to the dynamic form of the parochial constraint, we hypothesized that states represented on the military committees would benefit from higher levels of military spending. Since total military procurement expenditures are highest during periods of war, this is a rather direct test of the linkage between aggressive foreign policy and benefits to committee members' states. The military committees included in our study are the House and Senate Armed Services Committees and Appropriations Subcommittees on Defense and Military Construction. Figure 5-1 shows that between 1952 and 1972, the average amount of expenditures that states represented on these committees received increased by $25.2 million for each $1 billion of additional procurement expenditures.[b] This and the findings cited above suggest that the military committees fit the lower left cell in Table 5-1.[c]

It should be noted that the dynamic notion of the parochial constraint does not require that committee members' states average more of an

---

[b] The expenditure data were gathered from *Military Prime Contract Awards by State: Fiscal 1951 through Fiscal 1973*, Department of Defense—OASD (comptroller), Director of Information Operations. To control for inflation, all dollar amounts were converted to constant dollars (1967 base) using an index for industrial commodities found in *The Handbook of Economic Statistics*, vol. 28 (Washington, D.C.: Economic Statistics Bureau, 1974). The data on congressional committee assignments were obtained from the *Congressional Directory* and *Congressional Quarterly* for each Congress from 1952 to 1972. To obtain the parameter estimates cited in the text, we employed the Generalized Least Squares regression technique.

[c] Notice that we are not saying that individual congressmen from states that evidence this pattern of expenditures are in fact constrained to favor more aggressive foreign policies. To argue that would be an ecological fallacy. As throughout this chapter, our primary concern is with what it is about their states' involvement in military contracting that would constrain congressmen in this direction if they chose to respond to it. This latter choice would, of course, be subject to other considerations. For example, if one committee member is a dictator, the fact that other members are parochially constrained when he is not renders the constraint irrelevant. Similarly, a state level constraint might be ignored by a committee member whose district is not subject to it. These and other complexities of parochial restraint research are beyond our scope here.

Table 5-1

The Parochial Constraint on a Nation's Foreign Policymaking

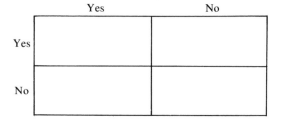

Static Parochial Constraint		*Dynamic Parochial Constraint* (Actors are constrained to expand total amount of expenditures to benefit their sector)	
(Actors are constrained to get more military expenditures than other Actors get)		Yes	No
	Yes		
	No		

increase per unit of change in total expenditures than do nonmembers' states. Nonmembers' states could average more of an increase and the committees would still be subject to a parochial constraint if, over time, a unit increase in the aggregate level of procurement expenditures resulted in any increase in the expenditures received by committee members' states. Only if an increase in the aggregate resulted in no change or a decrease in the amount received by members' states would the dynamic form of the parochial constraint be absent. In our analysis, a particularly strong form of the dynamic parochial constraint is evident: Whereas the average amount committee members' states received increased $25.2 million per each additional $1 billion of aggregate procurement expenditures, the average amount nonmembers' states received increased only $6.4 million per such increases.[d]

Conclusion

The study of whether parochial considerations constrain foreign policymaking requires careful specification of how in principle such a constraint would operate. In this chapter, we have suggested that the parochial constraint can take one of two forms. The static form is assumed in recent congressional research and two tests for it have yielded negative findings. But, if our preliminary analysis is any indication, the congres-

---

[d]This analysis does not consider the real impact of the expenditures received by each state. It may be that increased defense work detracts from alternative nondefense uses of local economic resources. It is unlikely, however, that the conclusion suggested in Figure 5-1 would be changed by this refinement.

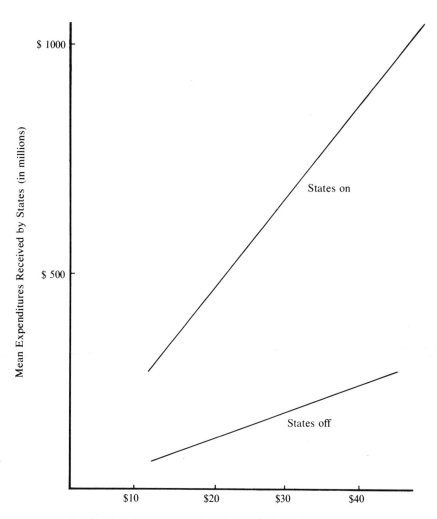

Figure 5-1. Shares of Military Procurement Expenditures, 1952-1972

Note: States represented on the military committees average more procurement expenditures when the overall level of procurement spending is higher.

sional military committees do seem to be subject to the dynamic form of the parochial constraint. This does not necessarily mean that the constraint actually affects the behavior of committee members—other things may intervene. But it does suggest that parochial constraint research should focus more on the dynamic form of that constraint.

References

Goss, Carol. 1972. "Military Committee Membership and Defense-Related Benefits in the House of Representatives." *Western Political Quarterly* 25:2 (June):215-33.

Huntington, Samuel P. 1961. *The Common Defense: Strategic Programs in National Politics*. Cambridge: Harvard University Press.

Niskanen, William A. 1971. *Bureaucracy and Representative Government*. Chicago: Aldine.

Rundquist, Barry S. and John A. Ferejohn. 1975. "Observations on a Distributive Theory of Policymaking: Two American Expenditure Programs Compared," pp. 87-108 in Craig Liske, John McCamant, and William Loehr, eds., *Comparative Public Policy: Theories, Methods and Issues*. Beverly Hills: Sage.

6

Legislator-Group Communications and Congressional Committee Decisionmaking

Kenneth Entin

Two traditions have characterized scholarly discussions of the role of interest groups in Congress. Group theorists such as Bentley (1908) and Odegard (1928) promoted a "mechanistic approach" that presumed group initiative and legislator passivity in the decisionmaking process. In contrast, the "congressional initiative approach," utilizing the modern tools of political science, has shifted attention to both the congressman as decisionmaker and to the linkages between legislators and lobbyists. According to this more recent interpretation by such writers as Milbrath (1963), Bauer, Dexter, and Pool (1963), and Scott and Hunt (1966), congressional attitudes and expectations help shape the context for group activity through the communication of cues.

The lobbying process is a two-way communications process that is designed to promote the interests and goals of participants through the exchange of information. In this complex network, competing sources vie for the attention and support of decisionmakers. The maze of decision points in Congress maximizes the opportunities for energizing these communications from bill drafting to final review. However, group strategies in influencing the content of legislative outputs must also take into account the uneven distribution of influence. Research has revealed both the importance of committees in decisionmaking and their role in filtering information for other congressmen (Asher, 1973; Entin, 1973). It comes as no surprise, therefore, that groups devote considerable time to communicating with legislators in a committee setting. What is surprising is that so little scholarly effort on Congress has been channeled in this direction. By examining the House Armed Services Committee we hope to help fill the gap in this relatively neglected area of committee operations.

Methodology

Data on congressional perceptions of interest groups were obtained through interviews conducted with members and staff of the House Armed Services Committee during the 91st Congress. The 21 respondents included 11 Democrats and 10 Republicans; there were four members with

43

one term on the committee, twelve with two to four terms, and five with more than two terms. This diversity of party membership and experience provided a cross section of interests and views that facilitated the analysis. The interviews, which ranged in length from 30 minutes to two hours, averaged 40 minutes. Minimal notes were taken during the questioning although a full account was transcribed immediately afterwards.

Data on private groups were gathered through the use of a mail questionnaire distributed from December 1970 to March 1971. Of the 34 sent out, 23 were returned. The questionnaire tapped evaluations of (1) the nature of their communications with the committee, and (2) the channels of contact most frequently used. Before examining the specific responses, the following caveats are in order. First, in the selection of a representative sample it became apparent that due to the broad ramifications of defense policy for all sectors of society, the classification "groups interested in defense matters" cannot be confined to military service and national security trade associations. A variety of business, labor, peace, and citizen groups has either a material or indirect interest in the decisions of the committee. Accordingly, an attempt was made to include each of these categories of groups in the sample.[a] Second, some military service and related trade associations do not register as lobbying groups as legally defined. Although spokesmen regard their associations as "educational" or "informational" in nature, this does not inhibit communications with members and staff of the committee. In fact, both sets of groups employ the same contact channels and share similar views about the process. Finally, the relatively small sample of 23 groups and the focus on a single committee obliges us to present tentative conclusions that should be reformulated as hypotheses and applied to other congressional committees.

The Context for Communications

Information flows to committee members from both internal and external sources. We refer to this multiplicity of sources as the legislator's "information environment." When members of the Armed Services Committee were asked to rate the components of this environment, the position of interest groups was relatively low.[b] Of 116 sources of information mentioned, only three (2.6 percent) were private associations. Comparable ratings were given to floor debate, the Legislative Reference Service, and

---

[a] The final sample of groups was placed into four categories: (1) *national security trade* (n = 8)—business associations interested in defense matters for economic (i.e., profit) reasons; (2) *veterans* (n = 4)—groups concerned primarily with the well-being of former military personnel; (3) *military service* (n = 7)—organizations interested in promoting the programs and increasing the budgets of one or all of the military services; and (4) *citizen, peace, and labor* (n = 4)—nonmilitary organizations with an interest in committee business.

the mass media. Most frequently mentioned were hearings, colleagues, staff, and executive officials. Such a finding seems to support those writers who have concluded that lobbying groups are not an imposing force in the legislator's frame of reference. However, the raw data do not reveal the intricacies of the access-seeking process. Information flows in indirect ways as well. Many committee members acknowledged, for example, that they rely on either the committee staff or their administrative assistants to develop contacts with outside groups. Staff members thus function as conduits or catalysts for these interests. The efforts of the latter are facilitated because staffers are more dependent on the information of private groups than are their employers (Milbrath, 1963, p. 209). According to one staff member, organized interests are particularly helpful in the preliminary stages of committee deliberations. "Private groups present ideas and serve as a vehicle for getting things established, such as justifying the necessity for hearings. In this way, they make an important contribution."

Members of the Armed Services Committee do not respond automatically to the entreaties of groups. Legislators communicate with colleagues and outsiders on a regular basis only if they respect their intentions and the accuracy of their information. If these are questioned, credibility will be strained and relationships may be damaged or terminated completely. Most interest groups understand this unwritten rule and make every effort to assure an accurate flow of information to the committee. The spirit and substance of this operating norm is captured in the following observation by a shipping association spokesman:

In many ways, a trade association such as————may be likened to a law firm. We of course represent the interests of our members (clients), for that in a nutshell is our *raison d'être*. But in representing these interests, we must maintain a certain ethical standard which, philosophical considerations aside, is quite necessary if one is to have any credibility with the Congress and the Executive Branch. And in Washington, as in the courtroom, credibility is a most necessary commodity for advancing your case.

Trust is maintained as long as the congressman's perceptions, attitudes, and beliefs indicate to him that he is not being deceived. The apparent consequence of this is that a member of the Armed Service Committee is likely to evaluate and react to a message in terms of the various biases that condition his behavior. Subjective considerations also determine, to a large

---

[b] The specific question was: "Assume you want to secure information prior to reaching a decision in committee. If you were to rate the following sources of information, which would you consider the most important, the second most important, etc.: hearings and reports; floor debate; personal or committee staff; conversations with trusted colleagues; Legislative Reference Service; executive officials (civilian or military); interest groups; mass media; constituents; other (please specify)." The total of 116 exceeds the number of interviewees because of multiple responses.

degree, whether a source will be even offered the opportunity to present information.

Committee members are more receptive to messages from groups with similar and reinforcing views than to those with opposing views. Eighteen of 21 congressional respondents (86 percent) concurred with this assessment although they were also careful to suggest that (1) all sides receive a fair hearing before the committee, and (2) lack of time necessitates this situation. Do organized interests structure their legislative strategies and appeals accordingly? Group spokesmen were asked if they tend to limit their communications with committee members who share their outlook on defense issues.[c] Of the 14 responses to this question, nine (64 percent) agreed that this is the case. The three peace and labor groups—those most likely to receive a hostile reception from the committee majority—emphasized the added burdens of an antagonistic environment. To compensate for their loss of access, they usually channel information to a relatively small group of committee dissidents. As a representative of a well-known peace organization noted:

In recent years 4 or 5 dissident members of the House Armed Services Committee have been extremely helpful. Otherwise it is a very difficult committee to work with for several reasons—the main one of which of course is the chairman.

Perceptions of Interest Group Activity

How do members of the House Armed Services Committee and agents of private associations evaluate the information provided by groups? To tap this perceptual dimension of the communications process, each participating legislator and group representative was asked a similar question about the flow of information to the committee.[d] On the congressional side, 16 respondents contended that little consequential information is provided by such groups. Those who shared this attitude stressed that the information services of private associations can be furnished by other sources. This posture is consistent with the low standing of private interests in the committee member's information environment. The remaining five respondents in the committee sample believed that the information service is important or useful. Not a single legislator described the information transmitted as "indispensable." The most frequently expressed view was that organized interests present a viewpoint, or more accurately a parochial

---

[c] The specific question was: "Would the recipients of the communications be likely to share the sentiments of your group?"

[d] For members of the committee the question was: "Would you say that private groups (or lobbyists) provide very little important or indispensable information to the committee?" Group spokesmen were asked the same question about their particular associations.

position, and it is the limited perspective and not the substantive information that is most relevant to committee decisionmaking. What is sought and provided is the specific impact of proposed legislative action on the constituents of the association. In short, committee members expect lobbying to occur but they do not believe it is a deciding factor in their final choices. As a veteran Republican on the committee noted: "They may induce you to take another look at something although they don't usually change your mind."

Past research has indicated that confidence in the messages of private groups is a function of party affiliation and committee seniority. Specifically, Democrats and freshmen members are more likely to react favorably to the arguments of group spokesmen (Scott and Hunt, 1966, pp. 63-70). Based upon interview responses, this generalization at first glance seems accurate. The five legislators who fit in this category are all Democrats and three are freshman first termers on the committee (see Tables 6-1 and 6-2). It is understandable that new members require a period of time to develop subject matter expertise and a "feel" for accepted committee practices. Until they are socialized into a system that promotes the internal exchange of information, relatively insecure newcomers are more likely to seek external support for their decisions. It is less clear why the high evaluation of group information should prevail among Democrats. In fact, a closer reading of the data for the Armed Services Committee indicates that party affiliation may not be the strategic variable. Committee rules and practices promote nonpartisanship, and differences with majority decisions are more likely to reflect disagreement with prevailing policy views. Understandably, therefore, the remaining two "deviants" from committee standards are "dissidents" who cannot accept the internal flow of information whose content is structured by the committee leadership. Since these legislators seek to avoid dissonance in their mental frame, they are forced to solicit information from sympathetic exogenous sources. A marriage of mutual needs unites them with peace and labor groups.

While a large majority on the Armed Services Committee places a relatively low valuation on the information furnished by private groups, the latter perceive their activities quite differently (see Table 6-3). Sixteen of the 23 respondents to the mail questionnaire emphasized that the information they transmit to the committee is either indispensable or important to intelligent decisionmaking. Thus, 70 percent of the groups as opposed to 24 percent of the committee selected either one or both of these categories (Table 6-4). The remaining seven respondents agreed with the prevailing legislative view that political decisionmakers can secure the basic data from a variety of sources. This judgment was unanimously asserted by the peace and labor organizations, a position that is consistent with their limited access to the leadership councils of the committee. By contrast,

Table 6-1

Committee Member Perceptions of the Flow of Information from Private Groups, by Party

| | Perception | | | | | |
| | Indispensable | | Important | | Very Little | |
Party	%	(n)	%	(n)	%	(n)
Democrats	0	(0)	45.5	(5)	54.5	(6)
Republicans	0	(0)	0	(0)	100	(10)

Table 6-2

Committee Member Perceptions of the Flow of Information from Private Groups, by Committee Seniority

| | Perception | | | | | |
| | Indispensable | | Important | | Very Little | |
Seniority	%	(n)	%	(n)	%	(n)
Low[a]	0	(0)	75.0	(3)	25.0	(1)
Medium[b]	0	(0)	8.3	(1)	91.7	(11)
High[c]	0	(0)	20.0	(1)	80.0	(4)

[a]Low committee seniority = one term on committee.
[b]Medium committee seniority = 2 to 4 terms.
[c]High committee seniority = more than 4 terms.

Table 6-3

Group Perceptions of the Impact of Information Transmitted to Committee Members

| | Perception | | | | | |
| | Indispensable | | Important | | Very Little | |
Group	%	(n)	%	(n)	%	(n)
Military Service	57.1	(4)	28.6	(2)	14.3	(1)
Business and Trade	37.5	(3)	37.5	(3)	25.0	(2)
Veterans	50.0	(2)	50.0	(2)	0	(0)
Citizens, Peace and Labor	0	(0)	0	(0)	100	(4)

Table 6-4
Committee and Group Perceptions of the Impact of Group Information

	Perception					
	Indispensable		Important		Very Little	
	%	(n)	%	(n)	%	(n)
Committee Members	0	(0)	·23.8	(5)	76.2	(16)
Interest Groups	39.1	(9)	30.4	(7)	30.4	(7)

most spokesmen for the military service, veterans, and business associations related their perceived essentiality to the direct or indirect impact of committee decisions on their constituencies. Since private groups seek to emphasize their importance while committee members attempt to protect their independence and initiative, it is clear than an exclusive concern with one side of the relationship would result in a partial and misleading conclusion. Overall, however, the data suggest that the primary activity of organized interests is to strengthen rather than change already established policy positions of committee members.

Channels of Contact

Special interests contact both members and staff of the committee. There are several reasons for interacting with the staff. Its members have long tenure, are nonpartisan, and enjoy acknowledged expertise. More importantly, frequent interactions with the leadership contribute to and magnify its role in committee deliberations. It is also more practical to see a staffer because a legislator's time is restricted by other pressing responsibilities. And, as noted earlier, the staff is more likely to give a sympathetic hearing to a group's case. Taken together, these factors help explain why an optimal group strategy is to rely on the staff as an indirect contact channel. A successful group's information will ultimately find its way to the committee through informal consultations, questions used during hearings, and in the committee report.

Group spokesmen acknowledged the use of various contact channels in their communications with the personnel of the Armed Services Committee (Table 6-5). Although certain techniques are employed by all groups, others are limited to specific types of interests. Lobbying and nonlobbying organizations both rely on similar channels. There is, nonetheless, a greater tendency for the "educational" and "informational" agencies to

Table 6-5
Contact Channels Used by Private Groups in Their Communications with Members and Staff of the House Armed Services Committee

Organization	Contact Channel				
	Testimony at Hearings	Personal Conferences	Telephone, Letters	Resolutions, Publications	Grass Roots
Military Service (n = 7)	4	3	2	3	1
Veterans (n = 4)	3	1	2	1	1
National Security (n = 8)	3	6	4	—	—
Peace, Labor and (n = 4) Citizens	3	3	2	1	1
Totals	13	13	10	5	3
Percentage of all Responses	29.5	29.5	2.8	11.4	6.8

Note: The totals exceed the number of organizations that answered the questionnaire because of multiple responses.

communicate only after they have been requested to do so, usually by the committee staff.

Of all the techniques used by private groups, face-to-face contact is regarded as the most effective way to present a case. Thirteen representatives of groups (57 percent) stressed the significance of hearings as a forum for the exchange of information, as did 18 committee members (86 percent). Representatives of interest groups placed an equal emphasis on personal conferences with members and staff. Understandably, the basic advantage of this latter channel lies in its flexibility. It maximizes the opportunities for compromise because it encourages informal conversations that are not part of the public record. The same reasoning underlies the less positive evaluation of the indirect contact techniques—that is, the group's position is less adaptable to shifting circumstances. Telephone conversations, telegrams, and letters are used by 10 of 21 groups but, in most instances, their primary purpose is to establish the groundwork for face-to-face contact. Group publications are formulated as instruments of persuasion by only five of the groups—primarily the larger organizations. Grass roots campaigns, designed to generate constituent activity, are considered the least effective way to inform members of the House Armed Services Committee. They are most frequently used during the consideration of controversial legislative proposals. Since relatively few defense issues in the past have been in this category, grass roots campaigns have seldom been used, and even then only by three groups in the sample, all of which are large national organizations.

Toward an Explanation

The impact of the committee on the behavior of all legislators is a fact not easily forgotten by group representatives with limited resources. If groups are to secure their legislative goals, then maintaining access to a sympathetic committee majority is a priority item. However, the stark reality for lobbyists who deal with a sympathetic Armed Services Committee is their relatively low position in the committee member's information environment. Research at the state level suggests that uncertainty may be a critical variable motivating legislators to tap external sources for information (Francis, 1971, p. 708). This observation suggests a possible explanation for the attitudes of committee members, since the decision process of the Armed Services Committee is highly structured and is designed to enhance its integrity in the House of Representatives. Although committee members are concerned with policy promotion (i.e., a strong military posture), they are not encumbered by widespread and successful challenges to the dominant viewpoints. This is due, in large part, to the bipartisan dimension of defense policy. It is also a consequence of a bipartisan collective leadership that serves as a reference point for less senior members. Democratic chairmen have made a conscious effort to institutionalize consultations with their Republican colleagues. As a result, senior members of both parties have been able to shape the flow of information within the group and also legitimate its most important substantive and procedural decisions. Group norms, including nonpartisanship, the emphasis placed on work in subcommittees, respect for committee expertise, and interpersonal trust among colleagues have furthered group rapport. By promoting cohesiveness, committee leaders have reduced member uncertainty thereby limiting the need for outside sources of information.

Other committees, most notably Agriculture and Education and Labor, have not been able to match this record. In the latter case, for example, partisan divisions have exacerbated the conflict resulting from contrasting policy orientations. Lacking a well-defined and accepted (i.e., structured) decision system, the members of the Education and Labor Committee have confronted greater uncertainty, and have been more receptive to external sources of support, such as the AFL-CIO for the Democrats (Fenno, 1973). A similar situation confronts the small group of congressmen on the Armed Services Committee who have sometimes challenged the majority on major weapons systems and policy views. For these legislators, the absence of support by the leadership or among their colleagues creates an uncertain operating environment. It is not surprising, therefore, that these legislators give the highest ratings to the value of lobbyist information provided to the committee.[e] The minority is forced to look outside the committee for guidance and support.

Committee members and interest group spokesmen hold contrasting views about the impact of group information on the deliberative processes of the committee. Specifically, 76 percent of the legislators argue that these exogenous sources provide "very little" consequential information while 70 percent of the groups stress the "indispensable" or "important" nature of the same information. The interesting and important question then becomes: Why the lack of congruence? A possible explanation lies in the differing operating assumptions concerning the nature of communications in the lobbying process. Representatives of private groups are aware that there is a linkage between the presentation of a case and the minimization of congressional dissonance. In practical terms, reinforcement of a legislator's beliefs facilitates access. Since committee members tend to deal

---

[e] During the 1960s, these dissidents met frequently with ranking civilians in the Department of Defense who were sympathetic to their problems. By soliciting information from a friendly outside source, they were able to present alternative viewpoints in the committee. However, their acceptance of committee norms helped maintain the structured decision pattern.

with sympathetic organizations, they come to expect an endorsement of their planned or present actions. *From the congressional perspective,* the transfer of information serves to legitimate decisions already made. Ironically, this situation reinforces the committee's structured decisionmaking system. Since the initial reference in the choice process is internal, subsequent external contact increases committee member confidence in the appropriateness of the prevailing pattern. The consequence of these attitudes is that the information role of interest groups is minimized.

From the group perspective, effectiveness is measured in terms of access. The primary aim, one which often becomes an end rather than a means, is to develop contacts with individual members of the committee who hold similar views. Once a committee member or staffer solicits information, it is perceived as a conscious effort to develop a *first line* of support. A friendly reception, positive feedback, and the dispensing of information are deemed the components of a successful contact. Groups consider themselves effective because they have been given the opportunity to present a case. For these interests, it becomes difficult to disentangle access, the final legislative decision, and perceived impact through the distribution of information. Since access is equated with influence, every effort is made to develop personal contact channels at the expense of the more indirect lobbying techniques. This unquestioned symbiotic relationship is functional to the smooth operation of the committee. It provides groups with an appearance of effectiveness and committee members with a reinforcement of beliefs.

The distinctive character of defense policy helps define committee member-lobbyist communications for the House Armed Services Committee. Only further research will provide clues to the relevance of this pattern for domestic committees. Variables such as subject matter content, perceived constituent interest, the degree of partisanship and the nature of committee leadership may have a bearing on the information role of private groups; the present effort also suggests the possible importance of committee integration. During this past decade, empirical investigations of committee decisionmaking have laid the basis for comparative analysis. A relatively neglected area—interest group interaction with a congressional committee—also deserves comparable development.

References

Asher, Herbert B. 1973. *Freshmen Representatives and the Learning of Voting Cues.* Beverly Hills: Sage Professional Paper in American Politics 04-003.

Bauer, Raymond A., Ithiel de Sola Pool, and Lewis Anthony Dexter. 1963. *American Business and Public Policy: The Politics of Foreign Trade.* New York: Atherton.

Bentley, Arthur F. 1908. *The Process of Government: A Study of Social Pressures.* Chicago: University of Chicago Press.

Entin, Kenneth. 1973. "Information Exchange in Congress: The Case of the House Armed Services Committee." *Western Political Quarterly* 26:3 (September):327-39.

Fenno, Richard F., Jr. 1973. *Congressmen in Committees.* Boston: Little, Brown.

Francis, Wayne L. 1971. "A Profile of Legislator Perceptions of Interest Group Behavior Relating to Legislative Issues in the States." *Western Political Quarterly* 24:4 (December):702-12.

Milbrath, Lester W. 1963. *The Washington Lobbyists.* Chicago: Rand McNally.

Odegard, Peter. 1928. *Pressure Politics: The Story of the Anti-Saloon League.* New York: Columbia University Press.

Scott, Andrew M. and Margaret A. Hunt. 1966. *Congress and Lobbies: Image and Reality.* Chapel Hill: University of North Carolina Press.

7

The Role of the Opposition in Foreign Policymaking

Sheldon Appleton

John Kennedy took office in 1961 hopeful of introducing some changes in a China policy he considered rigid and outdated. During his presidential campaign, he had argued against committing the United States to defend the offshore islands of Quemoy and Matsu against possible attack by Communist China. Vigorous counterarguments by his adversary, Richard Nixon, caused him to retreat from this position, however. And after his election, the die-hard opposition to any liberalization of China policy expressed by Republican congressional leaders seems to have persuaded Kennedy against taking any major initiative in this direction.

A decade later, a reorientation in U.S. policy toward China was signalled when President Richard Nixon revealed that he would make a "journey for peace" to Peking within the coming year.

In the spring of 1954, as the French position in Indochina deteriorated, Secretary of State John Foster Dulles and Chairman of the Joint Chiefs Arthur Radford pushed for U.S. intervention. But congressional leaders, including Senate Democratic leader Lyndon Johnson, opposed unilateral American action, and since Britain was also unwilling to join in the proposed intervention, President Dwight Eisenhower decided against it.

A decade later, President Johnson seized upon the Gulf of Tonkin incident to stage a retaliatory bombing raid against North Vietnam, and to gain overwhelming congressional approval of a resolution authorizing the use of U.S. armed forces in Indochina. Reelected by a landslide, in part by contrasting his restraint with the possible recklessness of his hawkish opponent Barry Goldwater, Johnson soon ordered a program of massive air strikes and dispatched to Vietnam an American expeditionary force that was ultimately to exceed half a million men.

These ironic pairs of events have drawn considerable comment, but McGowan and Shapiro (1973, p. 220) report that very few scholars have considered the possible influence of opposition parties on national foreign policies. Yet, events such as those recounted above, and others to be noted shortly, suggest that such study would be well worth undertaking.

Actually, the model put forward by Downs (1959) suggests the importance of the positions taken by opposition parties in determining foreign and domestic policies. Downs assumes that the goal of rational party leaders is simply to maximize their votes at the next election. According to his model, parties should not be expected to adopt the policies of their opponents, but to take positions that converge near the median of voter opinion on the issue in question.

Let us change one of the assumptions of Downs' model. We will assume that a state's policymakers have domestic and foreign policy goals that they genuinely value.[a] In order to implement these goals successfully, however, they will find it necessary to maintain the electoral or other support necessary to remain in office, and the legislative or other support necessary to carry out their policy preferences. Thus, it will be rational for them sometimes to sacrifice increments of legislative or electoral support for increments of policy goal fulfillment and, in different circumstances, to sacrifice some policy goals in order to maintain electoral and/or legislative support. This support, of course, may later enable them to implement other policy preferences, which may be more highly valued, or less costly in terms of electoral and legislative support, or both.

Foreign policies, as opposed to domestic policies, are generally less likely to have immediate and visible effects on the electorate. Consequently, a foreign policy decision or action not likely to have a tangible, immediate impact upon the populace and supported—or not strongly opposed—by the political opposition is not likely to be very costly to implement. A political leader whose foreign policy preferences coincide with those of the opposition will feel relatively free to adopt such policies, then, *whether or not* they fall close to the median of voter opinion. Further, when external events force a decision upon him, he will risk the least loss of legislative—and probably even electoral—support if he moves toward the position of his most effective opponents (i.e., those within or without his own party with the best chance of forcing him out of office or jeopardizing his other policy goals).

Another implication of this revised model is that we should expect it to operate differently in different kinds of political structures. In a parliamentary system with party discipline and a stable majority, legislative support for a government's policy program will normally be assured. Thus, the advantage to the government of preempting opposition policies normally will be greater in a presidential system, where the opposition may retaliate not only by calling attention to an issue through public criticism, but by acting in the legislature to make more difficult the implementation of the government's policies both on the issue in question and on other matters (which may be more important to the government) as well. In addition, we would expect parliamentary leaders to be more dependent than a popularly elected executive on the favor of members of their own party, and thus perhaps less free to take initiatives that depart significantly from the consensus within that party.

---

[a] This new assumption could readily be encompassed in the more general model expounded by Frohlich, Oppenheimer, and Young (1971).

To the extent that this model corresponds to the real world, we should expect governing elites in presidential systems to preempt the foreign policies of their most effective political opponents more often than their counterparts in parliamentary systems. A systematic exploration of this hypothesis is beyond the scope of this chapter. As a preliminary indication, however, we might look impressionistically at the postwar foreign policies of a few major democratic states.

In the United States, some actions consistent with our hypothesis, in addition to those cited previously, include:[b]

1. The Truman Administration's intervention in Korea and "neutralization" of Taiwan in June 1950, while under heavy Republican attack for "losing China" to Communism.
2. The Eisenhower Administration's liquidation of the Korean War largely on terms its predecessor had feared to accept, and its failure to intervene during the Hungarian Revolt of 1956, despite its talk of "liberation" in the 1952 election campaign, or at the time of Castro's takeover of Cuba.
3. The Kennedy Administration's reluctant implementation of the Bay of Pigs invasion plan prepared by its predecessor, and its forceful reaction later when it learned of the construction of Soviet missile sites on Cuba.
4. The Johnson Administration's intervention in the Dominican Republic.

U.S. policy in Vietnam might be dealt with by this model in the following obviously oversimplified terms (cf. Ellsberg, 1972):

1. The Truman Administration, under sharp Republican criticism for appeasement, initiates aid to the French.
2. The Eisenhower Administration, with an opposition less militant than itself, does not commit American forces to Indochina, and reluctantly accepts the Geneva Agreement legitimizing Communist rule in North Vietnam.
3. The Kennedy Administration, despite grave reservations, significantly increases the U.S. commitment to Saigon. Both Kennedy's 1960 opponent (Nixon) and the 1964 Republican nominee (Goldwater) can be expected to criticize roundly the "raising of a red flag over Saigon."
4. Lyndon Johnson initiates the Gulf of Tonkin "retaliatory" raids and, with the cooperation of Republican congressional leaders such as Everett Dirksen, escalates the war. This escalation begins to be reversed only in March 1968, when the candidacies of Senators Eugene McCarthy and Robert Kennedy for his own party's presidential nomination become the principal threat to Johnson's ability to continue in office and achieve his domestic goals. The president then renounces

---

[b]Pomper (1970, p. 188) notes that a majority of the promises pertaining to foreign policy included in the presidential election platforms of defeated parties between 1944 and 1964 were at least partly fulfilled, as compared with about three quarters of the promises made by the victors.

his candidacy for reelection at the same time that he moves toward his intraparty opponents' policy preferences by ordering a partial bombing halt.

5. Richard Nixon begins to liquidate American involvement in the war via "Vietnamization." (Perhaps the Wallace-Lemay candidacy induces him to move more cautiously than he otherwise might [Ellsberg, 1972, p. 98].) Truce negotiations continue, but bear fruit only when it is clear that the Democratic candidate in 1972 will be the strongly antiwar George McGovern.

A similarly impressionistic review of the postwar foreign policies of Britain, West Germany, France, and Japan yields relatively few cases comparable to those cited for the United States. The policies of the major parties in Britain have certainly converged, in conformity with Downs' model, but it is difficult to find many instances of a British government preempting its opposition's foreign policies, except, as in Labor's restriction of Commonwealth immigration, when a notable domestic issue was involved. Such critical decisions as Labor's decolonization and the Tories' aborted Suez intervention were moves away from the traditional orientation of the opposition.

In both West Germany and Japan, Christian Democratic and Conservative governments committed their nations to the Western alliance (the European Defense Community Treaty; the Japanese-American Security Treaties; acceptance of U.S. military bases; Bonn's rejection of the Rapacki disengagement plan) in the face of strong (in Japan, sometimes violent) objections by the Socialist opposition. In Germany, the Socialists' principal foreign policy initiative—Willy Brandt's *Ostpolitik*—was a move away from the usual preferences of the Christian Democrats—although, as often happens, their formal opposition may have been based less on intellectual conviction than on a search for partisan tactical advantage. The relatively rare dramatic turns toward opposition policies, moreover, sometimes came in political contexts unusual in parliamentary regimes: (1) since half of Adenauer's own coalition declined to vote for the reparations agreement with Israel in the Bundestag, its ratification was due to solid Socialist support; and (2) Japan's 1956 normalization of relations with the Soviet Union came on the heels of a party realignment in Japan following Ichiro Hatoyama's dependence on Socialist votes at a key moment in his rise to the premiership.

Results for the Fifth French Republic seem more mixed and ambivalent, as perhaps might be expected for a presidential-parliamentary hybrid.[c] Though it is not easy to determine who in France's multiparty system

---

[c]The Fourth French Republic does not offer an appropriate test for our hypothesis, since its decisions were often made by realigning coalitions and forming new governments.

constitutes the most effective opposition at a given time, de Gaulle's moves toward détente with the Soviet Union and recognition of China were in the direction advocated by the Left parties, which provided the most effective *electoral* opposition. His surprising acceptance of Algerian self-determination can also be viewed as a move toward the Left, but it could as well be argued the General's most threatening opposition at that time came from the Right. In other instances (the *force de frappe*; the withdrawal of troops from NATO), de Gaulle did not hesitate to use his personal standing and constitutional authority over foreign affairs to override the preferences of both Left and Right opposition.

In sum, this impressionistic review appears to lend some support to our tentative hypothesis. The purpose of this brief chapter, however, is not to demonstrate the validity of a particular hypothesis, but to argue for the construction of models and hypotheses that take into account the role of opposition parties in foreign policymaking. If the reasoning in this chapter is sound, then it is clear that the stance and actions of the opposition interact with other key input variables (e.g., constitutional structure, party systems, public opinion) in determining foreign policy outputs. Because of this interaction, further research on the role of the opposition in foreign policymaking is indispensable to the construction of any accurate model of the foreign policy process.

References

Downs, Anthony. 1957. *An Economic Theory of Democracy*. New York: Harper.

Ellsberg, Daniel. 1972. "The Quagmire Myth and the Stalemate Machine," pp. 42-135, in *Papers on the War*. New York: Simon and Schuster.

Frohlich, Norman, Joe A. Oppenheimer, and Oran R. Young. 1971. *Political Leadership and Collective Goods*. Princeton, N.J.: Princeton University Press.

McGowan, Patrick J. and Howard B. Shapiro. 1973. *The Comparative Study of Foreign Policy*. Beverly Hills: Sage.

Merritt, Richard L. 1973. "Public Opinion and Foreign Policy in West Germany," pp. 255-74, in Patrick J. McGowan, ed. *Sage International Yearbook of Foreign Policy Studies*, Vol. 1. Beverly Hills: Sage.

Pomper, Gerald M. 1970. *Elections in America*. New York: Dodd, Mead.

Part III
Foreign Policy Process:
Models and Research

Intellectual Dimensions of Foreign Relations Decisionmaking

Elmer Plischke

If the field of foreign relations is viewed from the perspective of its three fundamental components—the making of policy, the substance of the policy made, and policy implementation—decisionmaking applies primarily to the first and secondarily to the third element. Foreign relations also may be perceived as consisting essentially of the interplay of a panoply of those matters to which the decisional function pertains and the methods whereby determination respecting them is made. In either case, those responsible for the decisions must understand the nature and functioning of a spectrum of inherent basic and subsidiary factors that may be interrelated in various ways—and therefore may be graphically represented in diverse paradigms—and they apply their determining function at several phases of the process.

Foreign Relations Cosmography

One of the readily comprehensible and frequently employed depictions of the nucleus of the foreign affairs cosmography takes on a quadripartite configuration, with national interest, national purpose, national goals, and foreign policy vertically structured in descending order. Its principal advantages are its visualization on a single plane and its amorphous simplicity, but the latter, because much is left unspecified, also constitutes its greatest defect. All other items are implied, ancillary, or tangential, which, if specified in the formula, deprive it of its pristine and rudimentary character.

These four elements may be conceived—and often they are pragmatized—in the plural rather than the singular, however, and if the overall anatomy of foreign relations is to be made explicit, other ingredients need to be added, such as specific policy objectives, vital interests, implementation programs and procedures, national power and capability, and national strategy, as well as those organizational, institutional, and bureaucratic factors that relate to the making and effectuation of policy. While such a conceptualization has the merit of greater completeness, its main weaknesses result from the difficulty of interlinking the components logically and the impossibility of projecting them in a single dimension.

Contemplating the foreign relations cosmos from the point of view of the intellectual function of decisionmaking, its primary ingredients are depictable as comprising three main groupings or triads. At the epicenter lies the national purpose/national goals/foreign policy system. The third of these elements encompasses both policy objectives—the latter being more immediate and specific than the broader national purposes and goals—and the gamut of foreign policies that generally are defined as courses of action designed to attain the ends sought. The aggregate of policies may be stratified on the basis of importance—designated as primary, secondary, subsidiary, and tertiary—or on the basis of longevity—differentiated as largely immutable (strategic), potentially long-lived (intermediate), and essentially ephemeral (tactical). Policies may also be distinguished as both substantive and procedural. This triad, combining a chain of motives and means, is intrinsically hierarchical and even if its major constituents are extrapolated to their lesser, supportive ingredients, they may nevertheless be interwoven conceptualistically—but rarely are pragmatically—into a comprehensible, though intricate, fabric.

The second triad consists of the national interest(s) and vital interest(s)—which bear a coherent interrelationship—together with national strategy(ies) that involves planning to fulfill the interests, carry out the policies, and achieve the purposes. Execution of strategy relies upon the existence of national capability(ies) and the exercise of national power and often entails contingency planning and integrated foreign relations programming. The third triad amalgamates the host of organizational/ institutional, functional, and procedural factors that contribute to foreign policymaking and implementation.

While all of these segments may be intellectualized as essential to the foreign relations equation and need to be incorporated into a given decisionmaking consideration, because in their totality they cannot be projected on a single plane, they must be conceived as constituting a multidimensional complex. In this guise, the foreign affairs cosmography is a delicate network of separately identifiable but interacting components of various levels and priorities—in terms of either their inherent importance, their permanence, or their time relevance.

Those who manage the relations of nations and hold responsibility for making decisions are sometimes deliberately initiatory, but more often they appear to be reactive to external and other causal imperatives. Each action in the international arena evokes reactions, which in turn often become the actions that engender reactions anew, thus producing a cause-effect continuum involving a multiplicity of interrelations. Central to the process are those invested with the primary or ultimate decisional capacity. They are relied upon to perceive the issues, cope with the challenges, assess the possibilities, and choose among alternatives. Their discernment and judgment extend beyond the exercise of choice simply with respect to preferred courses of fundamental or occasional and immediate policy or action and affect, rather, the entire taxonomy of foreign relations.

Phases of Decisionmaking Venture

Much analysis respecting decisionmaking within this milieu of ideological, environmental, institutional, and other determinants consists of historical chronicling of past experiences, description and appraisal of the operational mechanism, or treatment of such more proscribed matters as legal prescription, particularized role playing, policy end product evaluation, communications flow, and methodological modularization. Little attention, however, is focused on the intellectual practices of policymakers and those who assist them in the exercise of their craft.

In essence, this intellectual dimension entails the perceiving, assessing, and choosing among alternatives—the central cerebral process whereby human minds are made up. Dean Rusk, Theodore Sorensen, and others have outlined the principal steps in the decisional process. Although, in practice, these may not necessarily be dealt with in a prescribed sequence, and some may be treated simultaneously or actually by-passed, normally they encompass separable groups of preliminary, central or core, and attendant factors. The initial phases involve such items as: (1) perceiving the decisional need, as related to the problem, the crisis, the challenge, or the opportunity; (2) framing the policy issue (and the very way in which it is posed may influence the outcome of the entire undertaking); (3) designing the assumptions (where essential or useful) and fixing the parameters, perspective, and focus of the consideration; (4) ascertaining, verifying, and evaluating relevant factual and assessory imperatives (including the decisions that must be made as to which perceptions become facts); and (5) determining the agents and agencies to participate, directly and indirectly, in the decisionmaking.

The axial steps include: (1) determining and analyzing rationally conceived alternative primary and secondary, long-range and immediate, objectives to be served by the policy formulation, and deciding on the preferred option(s) and establishing priorities among them; (2) identifying and evaluating rationally conceived alternative substantive policy solutions and weighing the desirability, feasibility, practicability, and possible consequences of each possibility, assessing the advantages and disadvantages of each, and deciding on the preferred option(s) or ascribing priorities among them; (3) defining and scrutinizing potential foreign relations methods and procedures, agents, and forums that may be employed, as well as timing relevant to the pursuance of substantive policy, and deciding on the preferred option(s) or fixing priorities among them, paying attention to possible use, simultaneously and sequentially, of multiple techniques and forums; and (4) reviewing alternatives respecting the form and timing of policy enunciation—both substantive and procedural—and deciding on the manner of pronouncement and communication.

The third category embraces such additional steps in the process as allocating organizational and functional responsibility for policy implementation, gauging internal and international reactions, evaluating the effectiveness of both the policy and the fashion in which it is instituted, and concluding whether reconsideration and modification are required. Although attention often is focused primarily upon the key steps of deciding objectives and the policies to achieve them, actually alternatives need to be weighed and judgments have to be made at each major step in the undertaking.

Intellectual Methods of Decisionmaking

In summary, in a single decisionmaking venture, multiple determinations must be made respecting the entire gamut of purposes, goals, and objectives, substantive and procedural methods of achieving them, agency responsibility within the decisionmaking machinery, techniques employable to execute policy, diplomatic agents and forums to be used, contingency planning, administrative management—and, eventually, policy evaluation. Such rationalization may be implemented by two basic operational methods—the advocatory and the options analysis systems—which are conceptually distinguishable and distinct, although in practice they may be joined.

The advocatory or judgmental method invests the decisionmaker with the aura of judge, and others advocate alternatives for his approval or disapproval. Unitary advocations merely require an affirmative or negative determination, and minor issues may be decided in this fashion. However, most foreign relations problems are sufficiently important or complex to invoke multiple advocacies, placing the decisionmaker at the vortex of a kind of multipartite adversary proceeding in which he exercises choice among the advocations presented and over which he may or may not personally maintain managerial control. Operating within an institutionalized government structure, this process usually takes on the guise of an hierarchical patterning, with each participatory level advocating recommendations upward and with the ultimate determinator comparing and balancing advocations in electing among them and arriving at decisions. Where the forum is highly bureaucratized, this is likely to result in a convolution of tertiary advocacies within secondary advocacies within primary advocacies—and many possibilities may be rejected or compromised before reaching the highest decisional level.

The options analysis method, on the other hand, poses the decisionmaker in the coalescing role of reviewing all important components and expedient alternatives concerned in the equation and of consciously managing the proceeding, rather than passing only on those considerations which are presented to him. It concentrates upon the systematic identification and articulation of all reasonable fundamental and supportive options pertaining to both ends and means, and the weighing of their desirability/undesirability, advantage/disadvantage, and feasibility/unfeasibility interrelationships—with the objective of rationalizing priorities among sets of possible choices and eventually of selecting the preferred option(s). It maximizes discretionary opportunity for the determinator himself by inducing, or at least permitting, the juxtaposition of an optimum menu of alternatives.

Application of Options Analysis

Options analysis may be utilized pragmatically, empirically, normatively, hypothetically, or historically—by practitioner or outside analyst—and by its very nature it encourages systematization of intellectual deliberation. It is applicable to the full range of foreign relations factors, problems, and developments, as well as to all stages in their progression that permit or require decisions to be made. It involves choosing among motives, missions, measures, methods, and men. It may be applied *de novo* to nascent or evolving situations or areas of concern, to a host of contemporary foreign relations problems as they emerge, to the entire spectrum of issues—or any specific question—concerned in long-range planning, to the preparation of various types of task force and other case studies, and to implementation procedures. It also may be employed for purposes of critical policy review—that is, respecting both that which actually occurred during a given policymaking venture and that which might have been the logical proceeding and resolution—and additionally, in the light of subsequent events, that which potentially could have been the best determination.

The decisionmaker or analyst may engage in options analysis by means of either or both of two basic intellectual processes. On the one hand, he may simply raise all the relevant questions pertaining to the matter under review and, in responding to them, arrive at his determinations. This method of "systematic query analysis" appears to be best suited to broad, general policy problems or to very precise and uncomplicated issues.

Alternatively, needing to cope with a complex subject, the decisionmaker may proceed to identify and judge among a variety of options rationally extrapolated, often on multiple intellectual planes. This may require more formal analytical structuring—or "cosmographic options analysis"—that can be achieved by devising a morphological outline or diagram of the pragmatized decisionmaking elements that is formulated on the basis of importance as well as time-sequence priorities. The principal advantages of framing foreign relations problems in the guise of such intellectual configurations are that the decisionmaker is impelled to view the components of his equation in terms of their interrelations and to arrange these in an integrated, logical patterning. An hypothetical model of the flow of interaction among the principal ingredients of the process is depicted in Figure 8-1.

Assessment

Depending on how it operates, the advocatory system of foreign relations decisionmaking may enjoy qualities of facility, practicability, and expedition. In view of contemporary emphasis on bureaucratic mechanism, power locus and flow, and political influence, it tends to be the preferred method, both in actual state practice and as a subject of scholarly scrutiny. If the ultimate decisionmaker remains uncommitted until the final stages of the consideration, he may be able to maintain an impartial judgmental posture, but he would lose the opportunity to direct the process so as to guarantee objective examination of all possible alternatives and to prevent having options foreclosed to him by the action—or, more likely, the inaction—of secondary determinators and avocates. Moreover, to enhance the quality of adjudgment, the policymaker who relies upon the advocatory system would need to guard against falling prey to the most recent, the least expensive, the less complex, or the more consensually evolved advocation rather than choosing the most meritorious option. He also would need deliberately to avoid permitting his decision to be based more on the persuasiveness of the advocation, or the personal or institutional power and influence of its exponent, than on the quality and efficaciousness of that which is advocated.

Such weaknesses of the advocatory system can be avoided if the primary decisionmaker either employs options analysis himself or requires reliable agents to exercise this responsibility in his behalf and then so administers the proceeding as to guarantee its effective operation. Otherwise, he may run the risk of succumbing to the most widely acceptable—which often means the most highly compromised and emasculated—determination, and the quality of the conduct of foreign relations

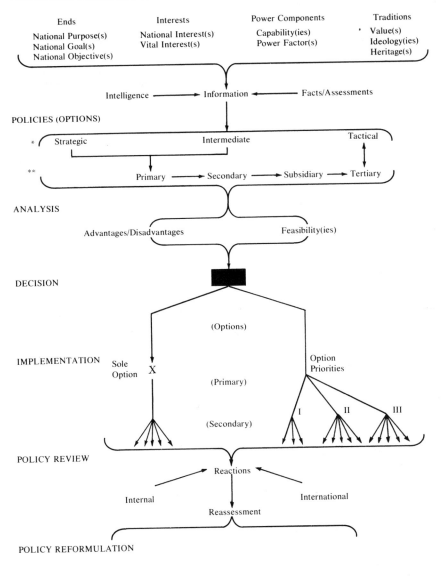

PRELIMINARY DETERMINANTS

Ends	Interests	Power Components	Traditions
National Purpose(s)	National Interest(s)	Capability(ies)	Value(s)
National Goal(s)	Vital Interest(s)	Power Factor(s)	Ideology(ies)
National Objective(s)			Heritage(s)

Intelligence → Information ← Facts/Assessments

POLICIES (OPTIONS)

* Strategic   Intermediate   Tactical

** Primary → Secondary → Subsidiary → Tertiary

ANALYSIS

Advantages/Disadvantages   Feasibility(ies)

DECISION

(Options)

IMPLEMENTATION   Sole Option   X   Option Priorities

(Primary)

I   II   III

(Secondary)

POLICY REVIEW   Reactions

Internal   International

Reassessment

POLICY REFORMULATION

*On basis of longevity/permanence.
**On basis of importance/significance.

Figure 8-1. Substantive Foreign Relations Options Analysis (Hypothetical Flow Model)

suffers as a consequence. While the two modes of decisionmaking—not being intrinsically incompatible or mutually exclusive—may be coalesced in practice, in view of the realities of bureaucratic politics, and because policymaking is bound to function most effectively only if the full range of alternatives is deliberately and fully considered and the ultimate decision is based on merit, care must be exercised to avoid an operational forum in which options analysis is simply presumed to be pursued within the advocatory process.

References

The principles contained in this chapter are developed more fully, with illustrative tables and diagrams, in:

Plischke, Elmer. 1973. *Foreign Relations Decisionmaking: Options Analysis*. Beirut, Lebanon: Institute for Middle Eastern and North African Affairs, Catholic Press.

This system of analysis has been employed in a number of case studies, including:

Irani, Ghobad Robert. 1973. "The Azerbaijan Crisis, 1945-1946: An Options Analysis of United States Policy." Ph.D. dissertation. College Park: University of Maryland.

Plischke, Elmer. 1968. "Resolving the 'Berlin Question'—An Options Analysis." *World Affairs* 131:2 (July-September):91-100.

_____. 1969. "Reunifying Germany—An Options Analysis." *World Affairs* 132:1 (June):28-38.

_____. 1971. "United States Southeast Asian Policy—An Options Analysis." *Social Studies* (North Carolina) 18 (Fall):18-31.

_____. 1969. "West German Foreign and Defense Policy." *Orbis* 12:4 (Winter):1098-136.

The following also are concerned with foreign policy formulation and decisionmaking:

Allison, Graham T. 1969. "Conceptual Models and the Cuban Missile Crisis." *American Political Science Review* 63:3 (September): 689-718.

_____. 1971. *Essence of Decision: Explaining the Cuban Missile Crisis*. Boston: Little, Brown.

Bowling, John W. 1970. "How We Do Our Thing: Policy Formulation." *Foreign Service Journal* 47:1 (January):19-22, 48.

Frankel, Joseph. 1960. "Rational Decision-Making in Foreign Policy." *Year Book of World Affairs,* xiv, pp. 40-66.

_____.1959. "Towards a Decision-Making Model in Foreign Policy." *Political Studies* 7:1 (February):1-11.

George, Alexander L. 1972. "The Case for Multiple Advocacy in Making Foreign Policy." *American Political Science Review* 66:3 (September):751-95.

Paige, Glenn D. 1968. *The Korea Decision, June 24-30, 1950*. New York: Free Press.

Rogers, Robert C. 1972. "The Intellectual Dimension of Foreign Relations Decisionmaking." M.A. thesis. College Park: University of Maryland.

Rosenau, James N. 1967. "The Premises and Promises of Decision-Making Analysis," pp. 189-211, in James C. Charlesworth, ed., *Contemporary Political Analysis*. New York: Free Press.

Rusk, Dean. 1965. "The Anatomy of Foreign Policy Decisions." *Department of State Bulletin* 53:1370 (27

Snyder, Richard C., H. W. Bruck, and Burton M. Sapin. 1954. *Decision-Making as an Approach to the Study of International Politics*. Princeton, N.J.: Princeton University, Organizational Behavior Section, Foreign Policy Analysis Series No. 3.

_____, _____, and _____ ,eds. 1962. *Foreign Policy Decision-Making: An Approach to the Study of International Politics*. New York: Free Press.

_____and Glenn D. Paige, 1958. "The United States Decision to Resist Aggression in Korea: The Application of An Analytic Scheme." *Administrative Science Quarterly* 3:3 (December):341-78.

Taylor, Charles W. 1972, *Panel Consensus Technique: A New Approach to Decisionmaking*. Carlisle Barracks, Pa.: U.S. Army War College.

9 Policy Studies and Foreign Policy: Emphases and Cautions

Stephen J. Cimbala

The policy studies perspective on foreign policy is both promising and sobering. It can safely be assumed that any new set of approaches will overcorrect for the presumed debilities of the most recent fashions. Thus, we are seeing a proliferation of studies, optimistic about our capabilities and imperative about our obligations to manipulate the "real world" of foreign policy decisionmaking.

There is a good case to be made for this apparent reorientation of emphasis within foreign policy studies, but the controversiality of such efforts has been exaggerated. Political scientists were doing this for quite some time before the postbehavioral revolution induced guilt feelings about quantitative methods, hypothesis testing, and rigorous explanation. The real issue is our capability to contribute to an enhanced science or art of statecraft by improving the conceptual apparatus of policymakers.

Much that is important in statecraft cannot be reduced to formulae or statistical nomenclature. Precise predictions about specific outcomes are elusive in the face of rapidly changing environments and policy contexts. Therefore, the decisionmaker will depend upon intuition and "dead reckoning" for certain choices. Making choices under conditions of uncertainty in international politics requires a subtle blend of skill, nerve, and accurate information distilled through the personality of the decisionmaker. What results from this process emphasizes the importance of *perceptions* in foreign policymaking: perceptions about the environment, actor objectives, and the characteristics of the domestic policymaking process.

Admittedly, decisions conditioned by perceptions of individuals involve the values of those individuals. It is unwise for us as scholars and students of foreign policy, however, to accept those values as givens and to offer advice to policymakers only about choices among marginally different alternatives *within* the same framework of assumptions. If we do not question the policymakers' assumptions we have allowed their perceptions to displace our considered judgment before the fact. Our particular facility, in questioning assumptions of policymakers and in disentangling their preferred patterns of inference, allows us considerable leverage without confusing our roles and theirs. What follows will elaborate on the dimensions of this policy-analysis nexus that are in most immediate need of further attention.

Immediate progress will require some limitation of conceptual and methodological foci. We cannot study everything at once, especially everything of interest and concern to foreign policy decisionmakers; nor can we surpass them at intuition or *ad hoc* improvisation. The more useful approach involves establishment of a conceptual and methodological core and some willingness to pursue investigations in that sector as a first priority. What social scientists have to say to policymakers *as social scientists* should be defined by the investigators rather than by their clients, although the clients retain their prerogative of acceptance or rejection of those efforts for their purposes. This recognition, of disparate prerogatives for producers and users, should not be confused with a defense of intellectual purity against the "corruption" of applied analysis. Some clarification of this distinction should be apparent in what follows.

First, the conceptual and methodological core of any policy studies contributions to foreign policy must fall within the domain of transdisciplinary behavioral science. This does not mean "behavioral science" as represented by its most committed reductionists, but instead behavioral science as a polyparadigmatic enterprise.[a] A polyparadigmatic behavioral science includes contributions from the comparative, experimental, and statistical methods.[b] Transdisciplinary behavioral study of foreign policy must also avoid using microbehavioral investigatory strategies to research macrobehavioral questions and the reverse.[c] Despite these qualifications, the interactive goals of behavioral science remain the causal explanation of relationships among phenomena *and* the control of variation among important policy-linked variables. The exorcism of explanatory ghosts must accompany improvements in our abilities to manipulate the real world, or we shall have no baseline from which to distinguish "improvements" from decrements.

Second, the conceptual foci of policy studies within foreign policy might emphasize the role of social science itself in public policymaking.[d] The scientific study of the role of social and behavioral science in public policymaking can be organized around the observed impact of "social facts," as created by the research of social scientists and as applied to problems by policymakers. By "social facts," I imply the products of descriptive, explanatory, and predictive social research that are incorporated within the interventionary conceptual models of policymakers. This is more than a convenience, and logically imperative, since social facts, as elements in actors' influence strategies, have mediated impacts on policy outcomes.

---

[a] This is very well articulated by Abraham Kaplan (1964).

[b] These are distinguished as fundamental strategies of scientific research by others (e.g., Johnson, 1974, p. 563).

[c] See Lowi (1973, p. 66) for a useful discussion of this point.

[d] See MacRae (1973) for a more extensive consideration of this specific problem.

The relationship between social facts and policy outcomes can be specified as *evolutionary* and *artifactual*. The evolutionary dimension (of the relationship between social facts and policy outcomes) depends upon the changing utilities of policymakers and political activists in their evaluation of social data. Given the existing state of our art, these utilities are subject to little or no control by us as investigators. The artifactual dimension of that relationship characterizes the nature of theory about policy outcomes and policy analysis, as understood and periodically reconstituted by social scientists. On *this* dimension we have developed monitoring capabilities and acknowledged evaluative responsibilities. The "creation of social fact" by decisionmakers is appealing as a focus because it implies that we should study *their* constructions of reality with a variety of tools. Case studies, simulations, correlational analyses, and even quasi-experimental contributions will be necessary.[e] The emphasis upon our understanding of *their* constructions of reality precludes escapism within sterile taxonomy and model building for its own sake. Working outward from a core of strength allows us to attack the periphery with concepts and methods of established effectiveness.

Third, the study of the creation of social fact by decisionmakers and our role in that process should be approached as a *scientific* and *applied* problem. The scientific issue involves the specification of relationships among variables that determine the construction of reality and interpretations of events by policymakers.[f] Here a "micro" emphasis has been most fruitful in the past, but hyperdependence on microanalytic strategies has pushed politics to the periphery of behavioral foreign policy studies. The applied aspect insists upon our commitment, on the basis of these investigations, to contribute to a sophistication and fine-tuning of policymakers' preferred models for understanding reality (Smoke and George, 1973). In this domain as well as in others, the best of "pure" and "applied" science must develop together. For this to happen, we shall need to tolerate some "sloppy" approaches and research strategies from the viewpoint of crackerbarrel logical positivists. It may be useful to specify an agenda of these, by no means exhaustive of all possibilities:

1. Adapted *outcome taxonomies* that establish clear distinctions among the preferred policy objectives of decisionmakers and the utilities assigned to various objectives;

2. *Underdetermined models* for description and explanation of the role of social facts in policy processes (as opposed to overdetermined causal models according to customary methodological canons of scientific

---

[e] Quasi-experimentation may be defined as a set of investigatory strategies designed to approximate the rigor of a controlled experiment within the constraints of real-world intractability (cf. Caporaso and Roos, 1973).

[f] Important contributions to our knowledge in this area appear in de Rivera (1968) and Janis (1972).

inquiry, which emphasize data reduction, a minimal number of powerful explanatory variables, correlational methods, and approximation of experimental designs);

3. Different *inferential* emphases in the study of policymaking activities, with new foci on policymakers' perceptions of important as opposed to trivial "nonnullities" (big disasters as opposed to small setbacks);

4. Explicit attention to the core *values* of policymakers and to the characteristics of political *institutions* that influence foreign policy outputs.

If the scientific policy study of foreign policy processes and outcomes can be oriented around these conceptual and methodological foci, where (more specifically) can we begin? Decisionmakers in foreign policy rely on certain sources of information, interpretive schemata, historical analogies, and inferential shortcuts that can and have been disclosed through various research strategies. Here our existing literature is quite rich. In particular, the cross-national study of elite attitudes toward foreign policy issues has contributed a data base that can suggest further hypotheses. Explicit reconceptualization of many of these studies and their findings in terms of the "creation of social fact" by policymakers is suggested as a next step. The comparative case could analyze the adoption by governmental bureaus of analytic methods fashionable within academic disciplines, and assess the consequences of these applications. As Campbell (1973) has noted, the feedback effects of these social science contributions of policy "amelioration" would be especially interesting as a milieu of investigation, if we could stand the heat.

Hopefully a policy studies perspective on foreign policy could isolate those impacts that we imagine we have from those influences that are behaviorally manifest. The *process* by which this behavioral manifestation occurs includes: (1) the *creation* of data and models by investigators in the social sciences who study foreign policy; (2) the *mediation* of these creations through the interventionary conceptual models of decisionmakers; and (3) the *repercussions* of these mediated creations on policy outcomes. This process and its constituent phases will resist any arbitrary distinction between the "facts" and "values" of investigators *or* policymakers in foreign policy settings.

References

Campbell, Donald T. 1973. "The Social Scientist as Methodological Servant of 'the Experimenting Society." *Policy Studies Journal* 2:1 (Autumn):72-75.

Caporaso, James A., and Leslie L. Roos, Jr., eds. 1973. *Quasi-*

Experimental Approaches. Evanston: Northwestern University Press.

DeRivera, Joseph H. 1968. *The Psychological Dimension of Foreign Policy*. Columbus: Charles Merrill.

Janis, Irving L. 1972. *Victims of Groupthink: A Psychological Study of Foreign Policy Decisions*. Boston: Houghton Mifflin.

Johnson, Chalmers. 1974. "Political Science and East Asian Area Studies." *World Politics* 26:4 (July):560-75.

Kaplan, Abraham. 1964. *The Conduct of Inquiry: Methodology for Behavioral Science*. San Francisco: Chandler.

Lowi, Theodore J. 1973. "What Political Scientists Don't Need to Ask About Policy Analysis." *Policy Studies Journal* 2:1 (Autumn):61-67.

MacRae, Duncan, Jr. 1973. "Sociology in Policy Analysis." *Policy Studies Journal* 2:1 (Autumn):4-8.

Smoke, Richard and Alexander L. George. 1973. "Theory for Policy in International Affairs." *Policy Sciences* 4:4 (December):387-413.

10

Reconceptualizing Foreign Policy Behavior: The Problem of Discrete Events in a Continuous World

Jerry B. Jenkins and William O. Chittick

In recent years, many students of foreign policy have been reading the newspaper in novel ways. The news is being classified, but *not* for the purpose of secrecy. On the contrary, the new ways of reading require the use of public coding devices to ensure that a variety of readers will be able to extract highly similar information from the same news source. Consequents of these procedures are the production of "event" data, "event" data sets and data banks, and, among students of foreign policy, an "event data movement."[a] These products result in other consequents for researchers in the area of international affairs. We believe the most troublesome of these research consequents to be resolvable, and the study presented in this chapter is intended to contribute positively to that end.

This study addresses the problem of what to do with information that, though originating in continuous foreign policy environments, is made discrete through categorization. We are not questioning the categorization process itself; that is necessary for reliably transmitting information among individuals and machines. What we *are* questioning is the failure to impose our conceptions of continuous foreign policy environments on the discrete manifestations of these environments that we have available in the form of "event" data sets. In other words, we are recommending that we consistently seek to reintroduce our machine-readable information on foreign policy behavior to the womb from whence it came. We make two such reintroductions in the present inquiry and arrive at markedly different results and conclusions from those of some event data studies which we feel warrant reacquaintance with a continuous world.

Foreign Policy Behavior: Conflictful or Cooperative?

Three of the better-known "event" data collections have been recently subjected to an analysis (Rosenau and Ramsey, 1975) that is supportive of conclusions previously derived (Rosenau and Hoggard, 1974) from only

---

[a] For a general survey of event data research, see Burgess and Lawton (1972).

79

one of them.[b] One of their conclusions is that the greater the international (event) activity of a state, the greater is both its cooperative *and* conflictful behavior (Rosenau and Hoggard, 1974, p. 132). Since the two analyses were of groups of countries, classified according to size, level of economic development, and degree of political accountability (see Table 10-1)[c] rather than of individual states, their results may not support such a state-specific conclusion.[d] Our concern here, however, is with the meaningfulness of the results themselves.

Table 10-2 presents the original expectations of Rosenau and Hoggard (1974, p. 134) and the results that are presently being questioned as to their meaningfulness. It should be clear from a cursory examination of Table 10-2 why the correspondence of conflict and cooperation emerged as a conclusion. Our contention with respect to the empirical rank orders for conflict and cooperation is that each of the two types of behavior needs to be evaluated according to the total distribution of actions that one country sends to another. Thus, if a country sends five conflictful acts to each of two countries, and if, in the same time period, it sends no other acts to one but sends 25 cooperative acts and 40 participatory acts to the other, we would evaluate the five conflict acts sent to these two countries quite differently. We would view the sending state as having a "negative orientation" toward only one of the two receiving states.

A formula for measuring the "negative orientation" of any state with respect to any other has been developed, with the assistance of Hardin Byars, and applied to each pair of states that are linked by an event in the World Event/Interaction Survey (WEIS) data collection. The time period from the WEIS collection that is subjected to analysis is roughly the same as that considered by Rosenau and Hoggard (1974) and Rosenau and Ramsey (1975)—January 1966 through August 1969. The 63 categories that the WEIS system provides for coding foreign policy behavior were, for our analysis, collapsed to five categories, as suggested by McClelland and Hoggard (1969, pp. 714-15). These five categories are: cooperative action, verbal cooperation, participation, verbal conflict, and conflict action. Imposing our formulation on the frequencies of actions across these five categories, a minus—or "negative orientation"—value can result as a

---

[b] The three data sets are WEIS (World Event/Interaction Survey) developed by Charles A. McClelland; COPDAB (Conflict and Peace Data Bank) headed by Edward Azar; and CREON (Comparative Research on the Events of Nations) led by Charles F. Hermann, Stephen Salmore, and Maurice A. East.

[c] We are indebted to Gary Hoggard for providing us with the genotypic country clusters.

[d] For example, if one of the groups consisted of two countries—one of which sent 60 conflictful acts and no others, and the other of which sent 60 cooperative acts and no others—there would be exact equality of conflictful and cooperative acts for the group even though there would be perfect inequality in the distribution of each of the two types of acts among the group's members.

Table 10-1
Genotypic Country Clusters

Large				Small			
Developed		Underdeveloped		Developed		Underdeveloped	
Closed	Open	Closed	Open	Closed	Open	Closed	Open
1	2	3	4	5	6	7	8
Spain	Argentina	China	Brazil	Bulgaria	Austria	Afghanistan	Bolivia
Poland	Australia	Indonesia	India	Cuba	Belgium	Albania	Ceylon
Russia	Britain	Pakistan	Turkey	Czech.	Chile	Algeria	Columbia
	Canada			E. Germany	Cyprus	Burma	Costa Rica
	France			Hungary	Denmark	Burundi	Dom. Rep.
	Italy			Mongolia	Finland	Cambodia	Ecuador
	Japan			Rumania	Greece	Cameroon	El Salvador
	Mexico				Holland	C. Afr. Rep.	Gambia
	U.S.A.				Iceland	Chad	Guatemala
	W. Germany				Ireland	Congo	Honduras
					Israel	Dahomey	Kenya
					Jamaica	Egypt	Lebanon
					Luxembourg	Ethiopia	Liberia
					New Zealand	Gabon	Malaysia
					Norway	Ghana	Malagasy
					Panama	Guinea	Morocco
					S. Africa	Haiti	Nicaragua
					Sweden	Iran	Peru
					Switzerland	Iraq	Philippines
					Trinidad	Ivory Coast	Sierra Leone
					Uruguay	Jordan	Somalia
					Venezuela	Kuwait	Tanzania
						Laos	Tunisia
						Libya	Uganda
						Malawi	Zambia
						Mali	
						Mauritania	
						Nepal	
						Niger	
						Nigeria	
						N. Korea	
						N. Vietnam	
						Paraguay	
						Portugal	
						Rwanda	
						Saudi Arabia	
						Senegal	
						S. Korea	
						S. Vietnam	
						Sudan	
						Syria	
						Taiwan	
						Thailand	
						Togo	
						Upper Volta	
						Yemen	
						Yugoslavia	
						Zaire	
3[a]	10	3	3	7	22	48	25

[a]Number of states by Genotype.

Source: Adapted from list provided by Gary D. Hoggard.

Table 10-2
Rank-Order Correlations for Rosenau's Expected and Actual Results

Rosenau's Conflict Expectations (Rank = Genotype)	Rosenau's Conflict Results	Rosenau's Cooperation Expectations (Rank = Genotype)	Rosenau's Cooperation Results
1	1	8	1
2	2	7	2
3	3	6	4
4	6	5	3
5	4	4	5
6	5	3	7
7	7	2	6
8	8	1	8
	$r_s = +.928$[a]		$r_s = -.952$

[a]The formula for calculating Spearman's Rho or the rank-order correlation is $r_s = 1 - 6\Sigma D^2/N(N^2 - 1)$, where D is the difference between ranks and N is the number of ranks.

function of a greater number of conflictful than cooperative acts occurring and/or the distribution among conflictful acts being more skewed toward deed than verbiage, than is the case for cooperative acts. Whatever the respective amounts and distributions of conflictful and cooperative acts, the greater the number of participatory acts (a rather neutral, but nonetheless nonconflictful, category in the WEIS coding scheme, including "visit," "comment," "consult," and so forth), the less the likelihood of a negative value resulting. Each case in which a state is determined to be negatively oriented toward another is included in Table 10-3, according to the genotype classification of the sending state.

By our operationalization of "negative orientation," we are answering the question posed in the heading of this section. If states are truly conflictful with respect to others, they are *not* also truly cooperative in their orientations toward those others. To fail to place discrete acts, be they conflictful or cooperative, in the context of the total amount and distribution of behavior that one state sends to another is to fail also, necessarily, to tap the basic orientations underlying the sending of any particular act. An example is the family. Most members of the family interact substantially more with one another than they do with nonmembers; at the same time, a disproportionate amount of their conflictful and cooperative behavior is with one another rather than with individuals outside the family. It should be clear, then, that we are not necessarily in disagreement with the conclusion of other researchers regarding the correspondence of the two sets of discrete actions: conflictful and cooperative. But that correspondence,

Table 10-3
Negative and Positive Orientations as Percentages of Possible Directed Links from Sending Countries to Receiving Countries and as Percentages of Directed Links Actualized by Newsworthy Events (from WEIS), by Genotype of Sending Countries

1	2	3	4	5	6	7	8	9
Genotype of Sending Country	Possible Directed Links to World	Actualized Directed Links to World	Negatively Oriented Links	Percentage of Possible $(4 \div 2)$	Percentage of Actualized $(4 \div 3)$	Positively Oriented Links[a] $(3 - 4)$	Percentage of Possible $(7 \div 2)$	Percentage of Actualized $(7 \div 3)$
1	360	115	27	7.5%	23.5%	88	24.4%	76.5%
2	1200	386	73	6.1	18.9	313	26.1	81.1
3	360	88	31	8.6	37.3	57	15.8	64.7
4	360	60	16	4.4	26.7	44	12.2	73.3
5	840	140	37	4.4	26.4	103	12.3	73.6
6	2640	212	76	2.9	35.8	136	5.2	64.2
7	5760	527	158	2.7	30.0	369	6.4	70.0
8	3000	190	65	2.3	34.2	125	4.2	65.8
Totals:	14520	1718	483			1235		

[a]Positively Oriented Links = Actualized Links (Col. 3) − Negatively Oriented Links (Col. 4).

where it exists, does not tell us much and, when not considered in terms of the context from which the behavior emanated, directs us away from, rather than toward, a determination of the basic orientations of any state toward any other.

Noninteracting States: Positive, Negative, or Neutral Orientations?

Having distinguished negatively oriented states from among all those that send conflictful acts, we wish to see whether there is any difference in the rank ordering of genotypes according to the distribution of negatively oriented states among them and the rank ordering of genotypes according to the average amount of conflictful behavior of the states they contain. We do this indirectly in Table 10-4 by correlating the expectations of Rosenau and Hoggard (1974) regarding conflictful behavior with two different rankings of genotypes with respect to the negatively oriented states that they contain.

The first ranking of genotypes by the number of their negatively oriented senders (Table 10-4) is more supportive of the expectations of Rosenau and Hoggard regarding conflict than is their own ranking of genotypes by conflictful behavior. The second ranking runs strongly counter to their expectations. Clearly, the difference between the orderings of the two ranks is attributable to one, and only one, thing: the denominator that is employed for determining the proportion of senders in each genotype that *could* be negatively oriented toward others (see Table 10-3 for the denominator values). In addition, our first rank is not only the one that is highly corroborative of Rosenau and Hoggard's expectations and results, it is also the one that employs the same denominator as that used by Rosenau and Hoggard in arriving at their empirical results. These determinations compel us to more carefully assess the respective meanings of our two denominators in Table 10-3.

Though each country in our universe of 121 countries *can* be a sender 120 times (or, stated differently, a single country can be 120 senders) in either of our two denominators and their corresponding ranks in Table 10-4, only if a state actually sends one or more acts to 120 other states is this possibility realized in the denominator for determining the second ranking. In contrast, the denominator that is integral to the first ranking does not differentiate between countries that actually send, and countries that could send, to others. An effect of this lack of differentiation is *not* to consider all nonsenders as being neutral (neither positive, nor negative, in their orientations toward others). Instead, all cases in the denominator upon which the first ranking is based that are in excess of the numerator are, by effect, treated as instances of positive orientations between countries. This

Table 10-4
Rank-Order Correlations for Rosenau's Conflict Expectations and Negative Orientations Derived from WEIS Data for both All Possible Links and Actualized Links

Rosenau's Conflict Expectations (Rank = Genotype)	WEIS Negative Orientations for all Possible Links	WEIS Negative Orientations for Actualized Links
1	2	7
2	3	8
3	1	1
4	4	5
5	5	6
6	6	2
7	7	4
8	8	3
$r_s = +.978$		$r_s = -.524$

is also true of the second ranking, but in that case there is some empirical evidence (linkage by event data) to corroborate the judgment.

Consider the implications of these considerations. The numerators upon which our two rankings in Table 10-4 are based are identical; they consist of all sender-receiver relations that are negatively oriented. All of these cases are also included in the denominators for our two rankings. Because there is no differentiation among non-negatively oriented cases, all of the additional cases in the denominators for the two rankings are necessarily considered to be positive orientations. This is not a problem in the second ranking because it is corroborated by empirical evidence. These cases in the denominator for the second ranking that are positive in orientation are, in the denominator for the first ranking, considered co-equal with all those cases for which there is no evidence (by event data) at all. To accept such a consequent would be tantamount to arguing against the empirical study of foreign policy.

Our reasons for rejecting the first ranking of genotypes in Table 10-4 should now be clear, but this does not entail acceptance of the second ranking. On the contrary, the denominators for the second ranking, by including only those cases for which there are event data, require us to assume that all excluded cases are equally neutral in their foreign policy orientation.[e] This is quite an assumption with regard to any pair of coun-

[e] When dealing with sets of *discrete* events, as in the analyses of Rosenau and Hoggard (1974) and Rosenau and Ramsey (1975), this assumption is required by the *inclusion* in the denominator of cases for which there is no information.

tries for which we are lacking information, and it borders on the grotesque when we consider the number of cases in the WEIS collection for which there is no information. The data in Table 10-5 inform us that fully 86 percent of the possible pairs of states in the world are not linked by even a single event in WEIS.[f] Furthermore, Table 10-5 reveals that there is a systematic bias in the distribution of noninteracting states among the genotypic clusters. On the one hand, only 5 to 10 percent of the small, underdeveloped states interact with one another; yet, they make up over 58 percent of the states included in the survey. On the other hand, 60 to 70 percent of the large, developed states interact with one another even though they make up less than 11 percent of the states included in the survey.

Thus, we accept neither of our rankings of genotypes in Table 10-4, for neither provides a reasonable answer to the question posed in the heading of this section. To obtain such an answer, we must, as in the preceding section, reacquaint our data with the continuous foreign policy environment of which they are a part. This is the task of what follows.

Reintroducing the Continuous Environment

Since the states that are party to nonevent dyads are not similar with respect to their attributes and their involvement in foreign affairs is not assumed to be equal, we introduce a measure of positive political interdependence of pairs of states that is not dependent on event data in order to say something more about them. With this information in hand, we revise upward both the number of positively oriented senders in each genotype and, by the same number, the total number of links from senders of each genotype. This upward revision is greatest for the genotype in which states have the highest average positive interdependence score with all other states. The upward revision declines, then, as the average positive interdependence of a genotype's states with all others declines. The revision is of information presented in Table 10-3, and the results are displayed in Table 10-6. First, however, we need to elaborate upon our conception of positive interdependence among states and its measurement.[g]

---

[f] We obtained the World Event/Interaction Survey (WEIS) data set developed by Charles A. McClelland and others through the Inter-University Consortium for Political Research. Although the WEIS data set covers events for 144 state-actors, we had attribute data on only 130 states, and positive interdependence scores for only 121 states. Consequently, the N in our study is 121.

[g] The positive political interdependence data used in this study are part of a larger data set developed by Jerry B. Jenkins under the auspices of a grant from the National Science Foundation (GS-42428).

Table 10-5

Number of Event Dyads, Number of All Dyads, and Percentage of All Dyads that Are Event Dyads, by Cluster

	1	2	3	4	5	6	7	8
1	2/3 66.7	2						
2	21/30 70.0	30/45 66.7	3					
3	4/9 44.4	19/30 63.3	3/3 100.0	4				
4	5/9 55.6	17/30 56.7	4/9 44.4	1/3 33.3	5			
5	15/21 71.4	31/70 44.3	9/21 42.9	6/21 28.6	11/21 52.4	6		
6	22/66 33.3	75/220 34.1	14/66 21.2	14/66 21.2	28/154 18.2	20/231 8.7	7	
7	42/144 29.2	143/480 29.8	40/144 27.8	16/144 11.1	41/336 12.2	57/1056 5.4	115/1128 10.2	8
8	20/75 26.7	73/250 29.2	10/75 13.3	8/75 10.6	11/175 6.3	18/550 3.3	54/1200 4.5	16/300 5.3

In the general case, "positive interdependence" refers to the mutual dependence of the actions of two or more actors where the actions of each are intended to make at least one of them better off in one or more areas of interest without harming any of them to a greater extent than they are benefitted.[h] The shared memberships of a pair of countries in intergovernmental organizations (IGOs) and their reciprocal diplomatic relations

[h] Interdependence, without the *positive* connotation, is defined as: the mutual dependence of the actions of two or more actors; the actions of either not only affect subsequent actions of the other(s). but are themselves affected by the anticipated response to them by the other(s).

are basically indicative of their positive political interdependence.[i] But, in assessing the positive interdependence of one pair of states relative to another, we ask two things: (1) To what extent is a dyad's political relationships (shared IGO memberships and diplomatic ties) as great as they can be and (2) to what extent do political relationships between a pair of states appear to be equally important to the members of the dyad?

The two ideas, expressed above as questions, are imposed on an NxN matrix (where N = 121 countries) that contains, in any nonmain diagonal cell, the number of shared IGO memberships of a pair of countries plus 0, 1, or 2 (depending on the dyad's diplomatic relations: none, unilateral, or reciprocal, respectively) for the time period from 1960 to 1965. With respect to the first idea, the number of IGO memberships plus 2 (for reciprocal diplomatic relations) of the most active country during any given time period is set as the upper limit on the extent to which a pair of countries *could have* participated in common during that time interval. By way of example, suppose that a pair of countries in 1960-1964 shared memberships in 70 IGOs (of 194) and had reciprocal diplomatic relations (= +2). Their "gross positive interdependence" with one another would be 72/103 = .699, where the 103 is accounted for by the most active country (France) being a member of 101 IGOs and, of course, having reciprocal diplomatic relations with one or more other countries.

"Gross positive interdependence," by itself, tells us "how much" at least one of the members of the dyad is dependent on the other. In order to estimate the extent to which that dependence is *mutual*, the second idea is imposed on the newly created data matrix of gross positive interdependence scores. The imposition of the second idea on the values of the second matrix generates yet another data matrix. The contents of this third matrix are "relative dependence" values that for any given dyad represent an answer to the question, "to what extent is one dyad member's gross positive interdependence with *all* countries accounted for by the other member of the dyad, and vice versa?" The greater the difference between the two percentages required to answer the question, relative to their total dependence on one another, the greater is the dependence of one country vis-à-vis the other, and the less will be their "positive interdependence" values in the fourth, and final, matrix relative to their "gross positive interdependence" values in the second matrix.[j] Thus "positive interdependence" will equal "gross positive independence" only when a pair of countries are *equally* dependent on one another.

---

[i] The machine-readable diplomatic and IGO data were obtained through the Inter-University Consortium for Political Research. For elaboration of the data, see Wallace and Singer (1970) and Small and Singer (1973).

[j] Continuing the example begun in the text, if 2 percent of one of the country's gross positive interdependence values is with the other member of the dyad, and the other's corresponding percentage is 5 percent, then we would have "relative dependence" = $(5-2)/(5+2) = .429$, and "positive interdependence" = $(1-.429)(.699) = .399$.

Having determined the positive political interdependence for each pair of states, we next determined the average positive interdependence of each state with all other states and, then, made the same determination for all of the states, collectively, in each of the genotypes. The latter result is displayed in column 2 of Table 10-6. Column 4 in that table provides our direct answer to that part of the question heading the preceding section that asks to what extent noninteracting states are positively oriented. Taking these into account, column 6 of the table shows the adjusted number of sender-receiver relationships that we are willing to make judgments about with respect to whether they are linked by positive or negative orientations. If one compares this latter column with the total possible links that exist among the states of the world (column 3, Table 10-6), it is clear that we remain short of judgment regarding the orientations among most of the states of the world. It should be noted that in spite of both this weakness and, somewhat paradoxically, the substantial impact that the introduction of the continuous environment has on our estimation of behavioral orientations among states, there is a positive .97 rank-order correlation between rankings of the genotypes according to the proportion of total possible links that are actualized by WEIS data and according to the proportion of those possible links that are accounted for by the adjusted links of Table 10-6. Thus, rather than turning the observable world upside down, we are simply including more of it. The effects of this increasing inclusiveness, and of reintroducing the continuous foreign policy environment are substantial, as Table 10-7 attests.

The predictions of discrete conflictful acts and discrete cooperative acts that are offered by Rosenau and Hoggard (1974) and Rosenau and Ramsey (1975) are shown in Table 10-7 to have virtually no relationship with either the adjusted negative, or adjusted positive, orientations that are attributed to the eight genotypes. This is not surprising since their expectations and predictions were formulated with respect to discrete acts, not with regard to acts in the context of the total amount and distribution of behavior that one state sends to another. At the same time, it is not surprising that a variable tapping ongoing relationships among states, positive political interdependence, should be as substantially associated with the nondiscrete dependent variables as is shown to be the case.

In this study we have argued that if we are to explain foreign policy behavior we must reconceptualize that behavior in terms of the relationships among the acts of any given state toward another. Further, once we have adopted this conception, we argue that our attention cannot be focused exclusively on the events exchanged among foreign policy actors without ignoring the bulk of what we mean by foreign policy.

The foreign policy relationships among noninteracting states are certainly not unimportant, particularly to the states involved. Indeed, the absence of event interactions in some cases may reflect the fact that these

Table 10-6
Determinants for Adjusted Negative and Positive Orientations, by Genotype of Sending countries

1	2	3	4	5	6	7	8	9
Genotype of Sending Countries	Positive Interdependence	Number of Possible Links	Number of Likely Links[a]	Directed Links, by Events[b]	Adjusted Links (4 + 5)	Adjusted Positive Links[c]	Adjusted Positive Orientations (7 ÷ 6)	Adjusted Negative Orientations (Neg. Links[d] ÷ 6)
1	.172	360	62	115	177	150	.847	.153
2	.193	1200	232	386	618	545	.882	.118
3	.126	360	45	88	133	102	.767	.233
4	.182	360	66	60	126	110	.873	.127
5	.103	840	87	140	227	190	.837	.163
6	.159	2640	420	212	632	556	.880	.120
7	.087	5760	501	527	1028	870	.846	.154
8	.108	3000	324	190	514	449	.874	.126

[a]Likely links (Col. 4) are a product of positive interdependence (Col. 2) and possible links (Col. 3).
[b]See numerators in Table 10-5.
[c]Adjusted Positive Links = Col. 4 values plus Positively Oriented Links (see Col. 7, Table 10-3).
[d]Negatively oriented links are given in Col. 4, Table 10-3.

Table 10-7
Comparative Rank-Order Correlations: Adjusted Negative and Positive Orientations with both Rosenau's Predictions and the Predictions of Positive Interdependence

Rosenau's Conflictful Expectations (Rank = Genotype)[a]	Rosenau's Conflictful Empirical Predictions	Adjusted Negative Orientations	Positive Interdependence	Rosenau's Cooperative Empirical Predictions	Adjusted Positive Orientations	Positive Interdependence
1	1	4	3	1	5	3
2	2	8	1	2	1	1
3	3	1	5	4	8	5
4	6	5	2	3	4	2
5	4	2	6	5	7	6
6	5	7	4	7	2	4
7	7	3	8	6	6	8
8	8	6	7	8	3	7
		$r_s = -.048$	$r_s = -.500$		$r_s = -.048$	$r_s = +.500$

[a]Rosenau's cooperative expectations were the inverse of his conflictful expectations.

relationships are developing in ways that both parties want them to develop. Can the student of comparative foreign policy afford to limit his attention to event interactions when these interactions fail to encompass all of the important foreign policy relationships among states? We have tried to offer a constructive answer to this question by demonstrating how event data can be supplemented, not supplanted, by the continuous foreign policy relationships from which they emanate and to which they contribute.

References

Burgess, Philip and Raymond Lawton. 1972. *Indicators of International Behavior: An Assessment of Events Data Research.* Beverly Hills: Sage.

McClelland, Charles A. and Gary D. Hoggard. 1969. "Conflict Patterns in the Interactions among Nations," pp. 711-24, in James N. Rosenau, ed., *International Politics and Foreign Policy: A Reader in Research and Theory.* New York: Free Press.

Rosenau, James N. and Gary D. Hoggard. 1974. "Foreign Policy Behavior in Dyadic Relationships: Testing a Pre-Theoretical Extension," pp. 117-49, in James N. Rosenau, ed., *Comparing Foreign Policies: Theories, Findings, and Methods.* Beverly Hills: Sage.

———— and G.H. Ramsey, Jr. 1975. "External and Internal Typologies of Foreign Policy Behavior: Testing the Stability of an Intriguing Set of Findings," in Patrick J. McGowan, ed., *Sage International Yearbook of Foreign Policy Studies*, Vol. 3. Beverly Hills: Sage.

Small, Melvin and J. David Singer. 1973. "The Diplomatic Importance of States, 1816-1970: An Extension and Refinement of the Indicator." *World Politics* 25:4 (July):577-99.

Wallace, Michael and J. David Singer. 1970. "Intergovernmental Organization in the Global System, 1815-1964: A Quantitative Description." *International Organization* 24:2 (Spring):239-87.

**Part IV
Foreign Policy Process:
Information and Actors**

11

Secrecy as a Reducer of Learning Capacity in the U.S. Foreign Policy Bureaucracy

Thomas H. Karas

A sometimes neglected cost of secrecy in the conduct of the United States foreign affairs is that it can hinder, rather than expedite, the effective formulation of policy. A comprehensive evaluation of the utility of foreign policymaking *in camera* would weigh this cost, along with the cost in democratic accountability, against the benefits of secrecy often postulated (cf. Wise, 1973; Franck and Weisband, 1974b; Dorsen and Gillers, 1974). Hence this brief chapter explores only a fraction of the issue: the ways in which secrecy can detract from effective policymaking.

In a dangerous, complex, and changing world, the ship of state needs a highly adaptive steering mechanism. The foreign affairs machinery requires a deep capacity to learn and to change course. The practice of secrecy, however, diminishes learning capacity. As Deutsch (1963, pp. 163-64) notes:

. . . the ability of any political decision system to invent and carry out fundamentally new policies to meet new conditions is clearly related to its ability to combine items of information into new patterns, so as to find new solutions that may be improbable in terms of their likelihood of being discovered, but relevant once they are discovered and applied. This ability . . . seems related to the combinatorial richness of the system by which information is stored, processed, and evaluated.

Detracting from effective learning are loss of depth of memory, loss of intake of external information, and loss of capacity for internal rearrangement (partial or fundamental). The practice of secrecy inevitably contributes to such losses, as presently will be seen.

Secrets are kept not only by the foreign affairs bureaucracy from the public and from foreign governments, but by elements of the bureaucracy from one another. To prevent the leakage of secrets, they must be restricted to the fewest possible officials with a "need to know." But, in the process, organizational memory and resources for the recombination of information are shut off.

In the Johnson Administration's deliberations on Vietnam, there was a "banishment of real expertise" as specialists were replaced by higher-echelon generalists because of the "sensitivity" of the issues (Thomson, 1973, pp. 101-02). In the planning of the Bay of Pigs invasion of 1961, CIA analysts could not make informed criticism of the Plans Division scheme because they did not have a "need to know." In 1941, military intelligence analysts were in part prevented from predicting the Japanese attack on Pearl Harbor because they were not permitted to know or see decoded Japanese diplomatic messages. They could not combine this information with what they knew from other sources because it was thought necessary to keep them from the secret of MAGIC—the breaking of the Japanese code.

Of nine "malfunctions" in presidential foreign policymaking described by Alexander George (1972, pp. 772-79), at least five are aggravated by secrecy and its consequent compartmentalization of information:

When advisers and advocates take different positions and debate them before the President but their disagreements do not cover the full range of relevant hypotheses and alternative options. . . .

When there is no advocate for an unpopular policy option. . . .

When the President, faced with an important problem to decide, is dependent upon a single channel of information. . . .

When the key assumptions and premises of a plan have been evaluated only by the advocate of that option. . . .

When the President asks advisers for their opinions on a preferred course of action but does not request a qualified group to examine more carefully the negative judgment offered by one or more advisers.

Although secrecy is sometimes asserted to encourage unfettered debate within the executive branch, the "Pentagon Papers" would seem to show that unorthodox dissent has hardly been a regular feature of classified policymaking (cf. Franck and Weisband, 1974a).

On the contrary, secrecy may protect rigidity, rather than flexibility, of thought within the government, because policymakers are protected from external criticism (see below) as well as insulated from external, alternate sources of information. Busy policymakers tend to value secret information as "inside," superior information: In 1962-1963, it seemed natural that the CIA and G-2 knew more about the Diem regime's military progress than did green young *New York Times* reporters in Saigon. In Deutsch's terms, secrecy promotes the overvaluation of internal as opposed to external messages (cf. also Katzenbach, 1973, p. 8).

Information intake may be limited not only by the properties of the communications network, but by the individual policymaker's cognitive apparatus. The presence of accurate messages within the body of classified information does not guarantee their use: President Johnson and his advisers seem to have ignored National Intelligence Estimates that questioned the impact of escalation on North Vietnamese fighting abilities (cf. Hughes, 1974). Such self-deception can partly be explained by the tendency of the individual to try to fit new information "into the pattern which he has used in the past to interpret information about the same situation" (Axelrod, 1973, p. 1248; cf. also Steinbruner, 1974, pp. 88-139). Various psychological mechanisms can discount ill-fitting data. Candidates for schemae that shaped perception and cognition in the Kennedy-Johnson circle of Vietnam advisers include (Thomson, 1973, pp. 101-02): China-on-the-march, monolithic communism, the domino theory, the inherent justness of an American cause, and the invincibility of American firepower and resources.

The culture of secrecy contributed to self-deception about Vietnam in two ways. First, it encouraged policymakers to ignore outside criticism of their faulty explanatory schemae. Second, secrecy sharpened the lines between insiders and outsiders, the knowing and the ignorant, the can-doers and the Nervous Nellies. Such a closed social system is extremely vulnerable to "group think"—the tendency toward a mutually reinforced, narrow consensus on a policy position (Janis, 1972).

Secrecy, then, distorts in a number of ways the processing of information in the bureaucracy. Another kind of cost it imposes is to place an extra load on organizational resources. Men and money devoted to the secondary activity of maintaining a security system are not available for the primary function of policymaking. The resource cost goes beyond the some $200 million spent yearly by the U.S. government to protect its foreign affairs secrets (as estimated by Moorhead, 1974, p. 102). Important as well can be the expense of executive attention devoted to preventing and plugging leaks and the consequent distortions in priorities on policy issues. The management of the Nixon White House "plumbers" unit perhaps exemplified such a distortion. During the also secretive Johnson years, one ex-insider reports (Thomson, 1973, p. 103), there was an excessive executive "pre-occupation with Vietnam public relations as opposed to Vietnam policy." It often takes lies to keep secrets.

A third burden of security maintenance is the occasional elimination of potentially useful expertise. While the Nixon National Security Council was trying to plug leaks, some officials were rendered ineffective by virtue of their being under suspicion as leakers. In the 1950s, some of the State Department's most knowledgeable China experts were purged as "security risks."

A fourth resource cost of the security system is the unconstructive intrabureaucratic conflict it stimulates. Bureaucratic conflict in itself is not necessarily wasteful—if it leads to the direct competition of alternative interpretations of and solutions to problems (cf. George, 1972, pp. 756-57). But secrecy lends itself to manipulation for bureaucratic advantage, since it sanctions the withholding of crucial information by some units from others (for examples, cf. Hughes, 1974, pp. 21-31). When secrets are not withheld for parochial advantage, they may be selectively disseminated, or leaked, so as to undermine the positions of bureaucratic opponents (for variations on leaking, cf. Halperin, 1974, pp. 173-89).

The limited intake of external information, the overvaluation of internal information, the tendency of closed systems to self-deception, and the limited supply of intellectual resources for the recombination of ideas into fresh approaches all might be subject to some correction by critical feedback, but it is just such feedback that secrecy most severely obstructs. Much is (properly) made of the value of the First Amendment in assuring the accountability of government and the self-expression of the citizen. More could be made of the potential contribution of freedom of information to the effective operation of government. Criticisms, suggestions, and alternative formulations of problems by congressmen, journalists, scholars, and other foreign affairs specialists might usefully correct the narrow perceptions, routinized responses, and self-deceptions sometimes besetting policymakers.

The wall of executive secrecy, however, doubly insulates the foreign policy bureaucracy from such correctives. Secrecy not only encourages policymakers to screen out external messages, but it prevents the outside specialists from obtaining the information that would permit *them* to form more cogent opinions about some foreign policy matters (and, incidentally, thus restrains full competition in the public marketplace of ideas).

When outsiders *are* given the "inside dope," it tends to be for one of two purposes, both of which maintain the isolation of internal thinking: Either information is selectively leaked to win public support for a position to which the policymaker is already committed, or else outsiders are invited to share (and to join in keeping) secrets so as to co-opt them into support or silence. The Washington press "backgrounder" sometimes combines these purposes (cf. Johnson, 1974, pp. 170-75).

In sum, a seldom recognized cost of secrecy in the management of American foreign policy is the constriction in several ways of organizational learning capacity. In an age of ultimate nuclear risk, of a fragile world economy, of ecological peril, and of changing distributions of resources and power, the nation may need all the learning capacity it can muster. This need is one of those which might be kept in mind when government secrecy is studied.

References

Axelrod, Robert. 1973. "Schema Theory: An Information Processing Model of Perception and Cognition." *American Political Science Review* 67:4 (December):1248-66.

Deutsch, Karl W. 1963. *The Nerves of Government: Models of Political Communication and Control.* New York: Free Press.

Dorsen, Norman and Stephen Gillers, eds. 1974. *None of Your Business*. New York: Viking.

Franck, Thomas M. and Edward Weisband. 1974a. "Dissemblement, Secrecy, and Executive Privilege in Three Democracies: A Comparative Analysis," pp. 399-441, in Franck and Weisband (1974b).

_____ and _____ ,eds. 1974b. *Secrecy and Foreign Policy*. New York: Oxford University Press.

George, Alexander L. 1972. "The Case for Multiple Advocacy in Making Foreign Policy." *American Political Science Review* 66:3 (September):751-85.

Halperin, Morton H. 1974. *Bureaucratic Politics and Foreign Policy*. Washington: Brookings Institution.

Hughes, Thomas L. 1974. "The Power to Speak and the Power to Listen: Reflections on Bureaucratic Politics and a Recommendation on Information Flows," pp. 13-41, in Franck and Weisband (1974b).

Janis, Irving L. 1972. *Victims of Groupthink: A Psychological Study of Foreign Policy Decisions*. Boston: Houghton Mifflin.

Johnson, Haynes. 1974. "The Irreconcilable Conflict between Press and Government: 'Whose Side Are You On?'" pp. 165-78 in Franck and Weisband (1974b).

Katzenbach, Nicholas DeB. 1973 "Foreign Policy, Public Opinion, and Secrecy." *Foreign Affairs* 52:1 (October):1-9.

Moorhead, William S. 1974. "Operation and Reform of the Classification System in the United States," pp. 87-113, in Franck and Weisband (1974b).

Steinbruner, John D. 1974. *The Cybernetic Theory of Decision: New Dimensions of Political Analysis*. Princeton, N.J.: Princeton University Press.

Thomson, James C. 1973. "How Could Vietnam Happen? An Autopsy," pp. 98-110, in Morton H. Halperin and Arnold Kanter, eds., *Readings in American Foreign Policy*. Boston: Little, Brown.

Wise, David. 1973. *The Politics of Lying: Government Deception, Secrecy, and Power*. New York: Random House.

12 Public Perspectives in Closed Societies

Richard L. Merritt

Any actor in a social system, to function effectively, must have information about its environment that includes other actors. Accordingly, modern businesses and governments often spend considerable sums to learn what their competitors are up to. Some of their intelligence activities are covert—once romanticized as cloak-and-dagger tales complete with *femmes fatales*, but now more frequently seen as a ruthless business with no room for sentiment. Some covert agencies or their operatives have even turned their talents to manipulation or "dirty tricks" as well as gathering information. Most intelligence operations are nonetheless quite above board. Governments regularly exchange envoys and tolerate attachés with the double function of transmitting their own country's views while observing and reporting on developments in their host country. Some governments also amass material on other countries from newspapers, statistical documents, and other publicly available sources.

With the rise of mass participation in political life came a recognition, slow to materialize to be sure, of the need to know something about the mood and likely behavior of foreign populations, not merely their governmental leaders. World War I, the first modern conflict to assume aspects of totality, was the watershed. Government officials began to see that popular morale was as important a factor in the successful conduct of a war as was the morale of the fighting man at the front. To further their political cause they undertook extensive and often expensive campaigns aimed at enlisting public support, both from their own and foreign populations.

Quickly realizing that their impact was limited by their scant knowledge of what the various publics really thought and how they might react to certain kinds of propaganda messages, these officials recruited new personnel who were experts on "public opinion" and investigated new procedures for getting better estimates of popular perspectives (Lasswell, 1927). In World War II, when "psychological warfare" took on "the character of a struggle for the attention, beliefs, and loyalties of whole populations" (Lerner, 1949, p. 8), Allied propaganda specialists went to great lengths to obtain the information about the enemy population's attitudes that they deemed imperative as a basis for their own activities. Such "strategic" information came mainly from interrogations of German prisoners-of-war and inferential analyses of current Nazi propaganda to the home front (e.g., George, 1959).

By this time, government officials and scholars alike had begun to attune themselves to questions about the roles played by the public in formulating and implementing foreign policy, as well as to the search for appropriate data on the public's perspectives (e.g., Almond, 1950). This task proved difficult enough even in open societies where freedom of access to relevant materials is substantial (cf. Cohen, 1973). If we are interested in the public's roles and perspectives in closed societies—as American policymakers and policy analysts were in the postwar years when they confronted the Soviet Union and its allies in the emerging cold war—then the research and analytic task is confounded by limited access to reliable sources of data.

And yet this kind of information is important. It can help to explain why the governments of closed societies took some of the actions they did, and why they did not capitalize on some of the advantages that they apparently had. It can help predict what these governments are likely to do in the future. If our purpose is to communicate with either the governments and/or populations of closed societies, then such information may tell us what themes to stress or avoid, how our arguments may be made more persuasive, what kind of impact our information campaigns are likely to have. It may even, by showing the extent to which our perspectives are shared elsewhere, affect substantive aspects of our own policies.

How can we obtain such information? Political circumstances did not permit the use by American analysts of newly developed techniques of public opinion surveying. So, too, inferential content analysis of messages directed at the Soviet population seemed less promising than had been the case with studies of Nazi propaganda: Soviet broadcasting and newspapers, indeed, the entire society, were under more comprehensive controls than was true in Germany under Hitler and Goebbels; and Soviet leaders were simply not under the wartime pressures conducive to the kind of hastiness, duplication of effort, and carelessness that had led Nazi propagandists unwittingly to tip their hand. An occasional visiting scholar might use quasi-systematic techniques to interview inhabitants of such countries (Pethybridge, 1967), but seldom is this encouraged by local authorities and, anyway, the scholar faces technical problems (such as sampling) that may seem to be practically insuperable. Excessive reliance on informants was, besides being risky, fraught with problems of reliability. What else, then?

This chapter explores three *overt* sources of information about public perspectives in the Soviet Union and East Europe: (1) indigenous public opinion surveying; (2) interviews with refugees from these areas; and especially, (3) given the fact that the other kinds of data are more widely known, interviews with East Europeans temporarily visiting the West. The focus is on *systematic* data that are objective in the sense of being independent of the personalities and intellects of those conducting the surveys, replicable at least in principle, and hopefully quantitative. This chapter emphasizes sources of such data, their uses, and their limitations rather than the substantive findings that emerge from their analysis.

Public Opinion Surveys

Closed societies have long recognized the need to know the perspectives of their own citizens. They have been more at a loss, however, to determine reliably what these perspectives are. Traditionally, they have relied on informants. In Nazi Germany, the state Security Service, under Heinrich Himmler, employed a network of informants who filed weekly reports on popular moods, rumors, and morale (Boberach, 1965); and in its zone of occupied Germany, the Red Army, after toying with sample surveys, adopted the same procedure (Halpern, 1949). Such methods, although useful, incur the danger that the informants are truly out of touch with their fellow citizens or else so anxious to please the authorities that they color their reports to screen out unpleasant news.

The advent of successful public opinion polling offered new possibilities. Indeed, a doctoral dissertation by a young German woman, who had studied journalism at an American university and become familiar with George Gallup's initial polling efforts, suggested that sample surveys in Germany could assist the Nazi régime to maintain effective control over the German population (Noelle, 1940). Although Goebbels never had the time (or perhaps the inclination) to implement the suggestion, other authoritarian régimes later gave serious attention to similar ideas.

Soviet bloc states in the postwar world have used or permitted the use of surveying techniques fairly extensively, particularly in the years after Stalin (cf. Ahlberg, 1969; White, 1973; Mink, 1975). In some cases, academic sociologists led the way. In others, including possibly the Soviet Union (Ahlberg, 1969), the need for useful data on economic behavior and consumers' preferences gave impetus to survey research of a more basic nature. By far the most widely reported data refer to audiences of the electronic media (Paulu, 1974).

Many such surveys, published in newspapers and periodicals (such as, in English, the *Polish Sociological Bulletin*), are of considerable importance for assessing aspects of society that form the infrastructure of politics. It is interesting to know, for instance, how people in western Poland are adjusting to their new lives in territories recently acquired from Germany; how particular concatenations of values make their way into local decisionmaking in Poland and elsewhere (International Studies of Values in Politics, 1971); how much time Hungarian and Soviet workers waste standing in lines to purchase food and how they spend their weekends (Szalai, 1972); or how Soviet youth views itself and society (Pozner, Filinovich, and Sherapov, 1965). The number of such sociological surveys is increasing from year to year, and the quality of their data improving dramatically.

More directly political surveys are not generally available to Westerners. For one thing, merely conducting political surveys entails certain risks. The prevalent attitude of mistrust would not have been conducive to candid responses. Moreover, what would social researchers have done with the responses should they have been both candid and negative vis-à-vis the régime? An Hungarian team, reporting on responses to questions about the underlying nature of relations among socialist states and responsibility for the conduct of the Vietnam war, took care to point out to readers which answers were "incorrect" (Mink, 1975, p. 212n). One might reasonably assume that the closed nature of society inhibits the openness of pollsters in the Soviet bloc.

For another thing, available data on politics are not likely to be reported in the press. The exception may occur when the results are generally positive from the régime's point of view. Overly positive responses nonetheless raise the eyebrows of Western analysts, who express (legitimate) concerns about whether or not the respondents felt intimidated, "loaded" questions, and possibly even slanted reporting (e.g., RFE, 1972a). Yet, it is not unreasonable to accept the proposition that the bulk of the population, at least in the Soviet Union, is in fact in accord with the basic principles and/or shibboleths of socialist society. We can then look for differentiation on less fundamental matters, following the thesis of V. A. Grušin, director of the Soviet Institute of Public Opinion, that "the absolute unanimity of opinions in socialism is accurate—and then by no means always—only within *certain limits*, only with respect to *certain* problems, and only in the framework of *certain* conditions" (cited in Ahlberg, 1969, p. 172; emphasis in original). With this caution in mind, analysts can better interpret the political data that appear periodically in the press of the Soviet bloc.

Unquestionably the most spectacular set of survey results to come from the Soviet bloc was a consequence of the "Prague Spring" in Czechoslovakia (Piekalkiewicz, 1972). The brief period of liberalization permitted several state, political, and academic bodies to conduct between March 1968 and March 1969 as many as twenty surveys that interviewed altogether about 35,000 people on a wide range of political and economic topics. Increasing political controls after the Soviet intervention in August 1968 led eventually to suppression of the survey results in Czechoslovakia, increasing apprehension on the part of both surveyers and potential respondents, and the subsequent publication of the results in the United States.

The volume summarizing and analyzing the data is understandably sketchy on some critical technical aspects of the surveys. Too much information about those who conducted the surveys, the author felt, might place them in jeopardy. Piekalkiewicz reports that "well-trained specialists" directed the surveying, that they spared no cost in carrying it out, and that, by and large, the response rate was quite high. The willingness to respond to interviewers jumped up markedly in April 1968, by which time many Czechoslovaks had begun to realize the genuineness of the reforms initiated by Alexander Dubček and his government. The rate fell correspondingly as repression set in again, until by March 1969 it was at statistically inadmissible levels no longer warranting continuation of the surveys. Surveys are marred by occasional tendentiousness, in which desired answers are suggested by the wording of the question. This is attributable perhaps to the lack of practical experience of the surveyers or else their own enthusiasm for Dubček's policies. Finally, again for security reasons, the author has neither published nor released documentation on the surveys. If we accept the published data at face value—and there is no apparent reason for not doing so—then we very quickly find that whatever their limitations, these data provide considerable insight into Czechoslovak political life during an extremely important period in its recent history.

Although the full range of data cannot be presented here, several points of interest nonetheless deserve mention. First of all, as suggested earlier about the Soviet Union, there was fundamental agreement in Czechoslovakia on the basis of political organization. Eight of nine respondents (89 percent) expressed their desire that Czechoslovakia should continue on the path of socialist development, as against only one in twenty (5 percent) favoring a reinstitution of capitalism. A mere sixth (17 percent) thought it even possible that antisocialist forces could try to change Czechoslovakia's political system. But, by the same token, solid majorities felt that their country should pursue its own path to socialism, and favored Dubček's liberalization. In mid-September 1968, several weeks after Soviet tanks rolled into Prague, three quarters (75 percent) of a national sample responded to an open-ended question about the most important condition for normalizing Czechoslovakia's life with statements calling for the withdrawal of foreign troops or restoration of the country's sovereignty.

Czechoslovaks revealed, in the second place, considerable diversity in their views on specific aspects of their political life. Asked about politicians, almost half (47 percent) thought that they merely promoted their own interests, another quarter (24 percent) saw them as "people just like everyone else," but only a fifth (19 percent) took the idealistic view that politicians struggle to carry out certain ideas. Over eight in ten (81 percent) wanted independence and equality for all political parties. Given a choice of various electoral systems, only one in a hundred opted for the present one, under which the communist-dominated National Front presents a single list of candidates for the electorate to accept or reject; asked to express opinions specifically on a continuation of the current electoral system, about a third (34 percent) responded positively and over half (55 percent) negatively. Beyond this the data reveal considerable variation on such matters as the desired role and composition of the National Front, choice of political parties, structure and tasks of workers' councils, emphases in industrial production, and collectivization of farmlands.

Third, the questions themselves indicate the kind of thinking that prevailed in official circles of the Dubček government. It comprised people who were willing to recognize that past solutions neither had worked perfectly nor were necessarily the most appropriate for the circumstances of the late 1960s. The sheer number of questions about attitudes toward the National Front and elections more generally reveals the interest of the government in finding out what changes might be most acceptable to the Czechoslovak people. In short, although it would be amiss to overemphasize the thoroughness of the Dubček reforms, the surveys strongly suggest that the régime was open to new ideas and information.

Obtaining the results of these surveys was surely a windfall benefit, as far as Western policy analysts are concerned, of the tragic outcome of the "Prague Spring." The surveys provide at the very least a benchmark against which to compare the more restricted findings reported in the press of the Soviet bloc, no less than the usefulness of other kinds of research approaches. They can be of particular importance in evaluating the results of interviews with refugees from closed societies or else their citizens who are merely visiting Western lands.

Interviews with Refugees

Using systematic interviews with refugees to explore public perspectives in closed societies derives from two separate but related intellectual traditions: cultural anthropology and social psychology. The first, which relied primarily upon interpretations of standard kinds of documentation supplemented by interviews with refugees or émigrés, was essentially a continuation of wartime studies of "culture at a distance," represented at their best by Ruth Benedict's analysis of Japanese national character, *The Chrysanthemum and the Sword* (1946). An example in the late 1940s was the Columbia University Research in Contemporary Cultures project that produced, among other things, an examination by Geoffrey Gorer and John Rickman (1949) of the peoples of prerevolutionary Great Russia. Another, "Studies in Soviet Culture," developed in the late 1940s under the auspices of the American Museum of Natural History, with support from the Rand Corporation. Directed by Margaret Mead, the project culminated in a wealth of insightful literature (the most general of which is Mead, 1951) on leadership in Soviet politics and agriculture, industrial organization, education, literature, and the new folklore developing around Lenin and Stalin.

Social psychological principles and techniques became an important part of the psychological warfare conducted against the Germans during World War II. One key element comprised interviews with prisoners-of-war. Now, interrogating captives to secure intelligence useful for military purposes was hardly a new development. It has been practiced since the beginnings of recorded history and doubtless before then as well. What was innovative was the use of questionnaires, clinical tests, and other techniques to get at more basic psychological variables that could help explain Nazi character and ideology (e.g., Dicks, 1972) or predict the German army's performance in the field (Gurfein and Janowitz, 1946; Shils and Janowitz, 1948). From there, it was not a great step to the postwar use of such techniques to screen Germans for employment with the American occupation forces (Levy, 1947) or even interviewing refugees to delineate Russian national character (Dicks, 1952), often by the same people who had deployed their talents against wartime Germany.

By the early 1950s, analysts had begun to use questionnaires frequently in interviewing refugees and quantitative techniques in analyzing their responses. One of the most important contributions of the postwar era to our understanding of Soviet life stemmed from such a project at Harvard University's Russian Research Center. Under the direction of Raymond A. Bauer, Alex Inkeles, and Clyde Kluckhohn, the Harvard Project on the Soviet Social System obtained responses to general questionnaires from 2,718 Soviet émigrés in West Germany, Austria, and the eastern United States; 9,748 written questionnaires on special topics; 329 extended life-history interviews and 435 interviews on special topics; and 60 depth interviews that included clinical psychological tests. The wide-ranging results appeared in a plethora of monographs that dealt with such topics as cultural, psychological, and social themes in the Soviet system (Bauer, Inkeles, and Kluckhohn, 1957), daily life (Inkeles and Bauer, 1959), and the family (Geiger, 1968).

Subsequent studies surveyed the views of refugees from states that fell under communist domination after World War II. One of the more interesting of these, conducted in behalf of the United States Information Agency by a commerical firm, International Public Opinion Research, Inc., comprised 300 interviews in 1950-51 with Czechoslovak, Hungarian, and Polish refugees who had been in the West for only weeks or, in some cases, days (IPOR, 1953; cf., for a nonquantitative analysis, Kracauer and Berkman, 1956). It was among the first studies to demonstrate empirically that the bulk of later refugees had not defected for political or ideological reasons, but because they were weary of their countries' poor living conditions and, often due to special circumstances, were actually in a position to flee without taking inordinate risks.

Other such research projects followed. American authorities in semisovereign Germany and Radio Free Europe frequently interviewed refugees from East Germany or other parts of the Soviet bloc. In 1954-56, a commercial surveying firm in Munich, Infratest, under contract to the West German Federal Ministry for All-German Affairs, interviewed young people, factory workers, white-collar employees, and others who had recently departed the German Democratic Republic. The study on youth (Schröter, 1958), for instance, administered questionnaires to 558 refugees between the ages of 15 and 24—a representative sample of the roughly 220,000 youths who had fled during the period when interviewing took place—to find out about both their views on the system they had left and the problems they were encountering in integrating themselves into West German society. Interviews during the year after the Hungarian uprising of 1956 with 95 refugees who had migrated to the United States found intense and often active hostility to their former régime, but considerably less agreement on what should replace it (Gleitman and Greenbaum, 1960). On the other side of the world, Solomon (1971) used interviews with 91 émigrés to develop an extensive analysis of Chinese political culture.

Intuitively, it would seem that interviews with refugees and émigrés pose virtually insurmountable analytic problems: The respondents are not likely to be a representative sample of the population that they left behind, their information is apt to be out of date, and their responses biased against their former country either to justify their own decision to flee or to ingratiate themselves with the interviewer who, the respondents may assume, wants to hear the worst about their former homeland. The most carefully considered response to such objections was formulated by the Harvard Project (Inkeles and Bauer, 1959, pp. 3-64). Comparison of relevant subsamples within the entire set of respondents and internal checks on the validity of responses (e.g., a "flattery scale" designed to ascertain which respondents were merely trying to please) suggested that problems deriving from sampling procedures or responses that were less than candid were, although by no means trivial, not so great as had been anticipated, nor did they preclude meaningful analysis of the results. Indeed, by taking account of the discrepancies, the analysts were forced to spell out more clearly than might otherwise have been done both the limits as well as possibilities of interpretation.

Focusing on more recent arrivals to the West mitigates some of the problems mentioned above. Recent refugees are likely to have current information, for one thing. Moreover, analysts, by working closely with refugee reception centers, can obtain a more representative sample of those who actually flee (or at least register themselves as refugees). The IPOR project, for instance, interviewed "nearly every Pole who came into Germany and nearly every Hungarian and Czech who came into the American Zone of Austria" during the winter months of 1951-52 (Sheldon and Dutkowski, 1952-53; cf. IPOR, 1953). But, however representative of *refugees* the sample may be, it continues to be unrepresentative of the *home population* because of a virtual absence of communists or others who are happy with the régime, as well as those who lack the courage or, more importantly, opportunity to defect.

Judicious use of data deriving from interviews with refugees, problematic though the data may be, can nevertheless add to our understanding of life in closed societies. Sampling biases, such as overrepresentation of workers and peasants and concomitant underrepresentation of communists in the IPOR sample, prohibit a simple extrapolation of findings on reported behavior to a broader population unless its characteristics are known in sufficient detail to permit assigning weights within the sample. Still, the data can show dimensions of popular perspectives, and they can show changes over time in these dimensions, even if the precise distribution of the perspectives is not known.

Visitors to the West

Another potential source of relevant information comprises visitors from closed societies. The case for interviewing such people is strong. Like recent refugees—but unlike many respondents in the studies discussed previously, who had spent long periods in various camps for displaced persons—visitors are likely to be freshly arrived and hence *au courant* in their knowledge of what is happening in the home country. They are likely to enjoy a vast network of primary and other ties to the area they came from. And, since they are merely temporarily in the West to attend a trade fair, participate in a scientific congress, visit a gravely ill relative, or simply see the sights, they will presumably return home in the near future and are thus apt to see their country in terms of the future as well as the past.

By the same token, however, the visitor to the West is hardly the typical citizen of the closed society. During the heyday of Stalinism, such visitors appeared rarely at Western functions, and those who did seemed particularly conscious of pressures on them to behave in ways approved by the régime. There is no reason to assume a priori that such visitors since the mid-1950s have been any more representative of their compatriots. What evidence is available indicates rather that visitors are likely to be more highly educated, more mobile socially, and in more responsible positions than those who do not travel to the West.

Research teams interviewing visitors to the West and reporting their findings have been sharply aware of the potential bias deriving from the lack of complete representativeness. As in the case of interviews with refugees, the key questions become rather: How can the consequences of such variations be accurately assessed? What use can be made of the resulting data, while taking into account inherent limitations? Some answers to these questions are provided by the findings of two major organizations that have interviewed visitors (as well as refugees) on a continuing basis: the United States Department of State and Radio Free Europe (supported with a heavy dose of United States governmental funds).

HICOG Studies

Berlin of the 1950s provided a unique opportunity for American officials to gain insights into the perspectives and behavior of East Germans. When the Berlin blockade was lifted in May 1949, Germans found that their country was to all intents and purposes formally divided into the Federal Republic (FRG) in the west and the German Democratic Republic (GDR) in the east, and so, too, was their former capital city of Berlin. Access between East and West Berlin nonetheless remained fairly free. This situation, which ended in August 1961 with the construction of the Berlin wall, permitted Americans to make direct observations in the eastern portion of the city and East Berliners and other GDR citizens to visit friends and relatives, shop, attend the theater and other public events, and even find employment in West Berlin.

In August 1950, the Reaction Analysis Staff, Office of Public Affairs, Office of the U.S. High Commissioner for Germany (HICOG) turned its attention for the first time to East Germans visiting West Berlin. The staff and its predecessor during the military government era had been surveying German attitudes virtually since the first American troops entered Germany in early 1945 (Merritt and Merritt, 1970). Between 1950 and 1958, in addition to its more frequent and exhaustive surveys of West Germans and West Berliners, it conducted at least 24 separate samplings of East German views on such diverse topics as life in the GDR, expectations of German unification, the relationship between the United States and the Soviet Union, and favorite radio stations (Merritt and Merritt, forthcoming).

Technical problems encountered in conducting the surveys were formidable. Not least of these was locating East Germans. Initial efforts centered on such sites as currency exchanges and shopping areas, but by 1951 HICOG surveyers had set a pattern of interviewing East Germans attending the annual industrial fair in the fall and the agricultural fair in late winter. Sometimes other opportunities presented themselves as well: visits to reception centers in West Berlin by young people who were attending an East Berlin youth festival in August 1951, to food distribution centers set up in West Berlin after the East German uprising of June 1953, and to the international architectural exhibit in the Hansa Quarter of West Berlin in summer 1957. Generally, the industrial and agricultural fairs were best, since the surveyers could count on visits by several hundred thousand East Germans to each during the period of one or two weeks.

Another problem was the approach to be used in soliciting interviews. Initially, the German interviewers working for HICOG acknowledged United States sponsorship in some cases, but the difference that knowledge of sponsorhip made in the responses was sufficiently slight that HICOG officials finally instructed their interviewers to report merely that the survey was being conducted under the (presumably neutral-sounding) auspices of the "Institute for Opinion Research." Eventually, the entire task was turned over on a contractual basis to a commercial firm wholly owned and operated by Germans. Early surveys found between a tenth and a fifth of the prospective respondents refusing interviews, possibly because of a fear that they were being watched or that the interviewers were GDR agents in disguise, or else possibly because they feared that interviewers were Western agents, contact with whom could be compromising. (And, indeed, East German sources did warn that Western pollsters were es-pionage agents; see Halpern, 1949). Conducting interviews in private rooms at a large public event, such as the industrial fair, seemed to allay such fears, thereby producing higher response rates.

Ultimately, however, the key question for the surveyers was the valid-ity of the sample. Once they secured reliable information on the GDR's population structure, it was possible to establish quotas (according to geographic region, sex, and sometimes age) to guide the interviewers' selection of potential respondents. What they could not control for was the distribution of the respondents' attitudinal and behavioral predispositions. A survey of spectators at a pornographic moviehouse in an American town may well be representative of those actually attending the movie, but not all groups in the community are equally likely to attend the movie in the first place. Similarly, for whatever reasons, individual East Germans were not equally likely to visit the exhibition center in West Berlin.

HICOG officials made some attempts if not to validate their samples at least to determine how they compared to other samples—notably West Germans and refugees from the GDR. Comparisons with West Berliners and West Germans showed that they all focused their attention on the same things, but viewed them somewhat differently and that, if anything, the East Germans were more pessimistic about the future of East-West rela-tions and prospects for German reunification than were those from the West. A similar comparison with responses of refugees reveals few statistically significant differences, with most of these accounted for by the low level of the refugees' information. In the remaining cases, the refugees were simply more critical of the governments' behavior—East and West alike—on such questions as the reunification of Germany. These tests, however interesting, did not validate the sample of GDR respondents as being representative of the entire GDR population in terms of attitudinal and behavioral predispositions. The nagging doubt remained of how much bias the data contained. The best that HICOG reporters could say, finally, was that their readers had to bear in mind the limitations of the data when evaluating them.

RFE Surveys

Still another set of studies rested on interviews with visitors to the West from other countries in the Soviet bloc. Perhaps the best known of these is the continuing series conducted by the Audience and Public Opinion Research Department, Radio Free Europe. Although in earlier years RFE necessarily concentrated on refugees, the opening of easier relations between East and West permitted its surveying instead to concentrate on East European businessmen, conventioneers, tourists, and others temporarily in West Europe. RFE reports, alas, give only the most basic information about the sample and none at all about the procedures used in identifying and approaching prospective respondents. Surveying is on a continuing basis, with cumulated data for a particular time span reported periodically.

A primary purpose of the surveys is to ascertain the extent to which East Europeans listen to RFE radio broadcasts. Many also deal with such topical issues as crises in the Middle East, views of the superpowers, Soviet intervention in Czechoslovakia in 1968, American intervention in Vietnam, major concerns facing the respondents' countries, West Germany's eastern policy under Chancellor Willy Brandt, the European Security Conference, and how the respondents would vote if free elections were to be held in their countries.

Occasional releases of public opinion data from Poland and Czechoslovakia have permitted RFE surveyers to check the validity of their own findings. It would seem that RFE respondents are more alert than are "average Poles" to the media, particularly the radio (RFE, 1972b) but also the newspapers (RFE, 1967b); it may also be that Polish respondents are unwilling to report to Polish pollsters certain kinds of programs (and unregistered transistor radios) to which they listen (RFE, 1972c). A slight difference in Polish expectations of war between East and West seems best accounted for by variations in the wording of the questions (RFE, 1971). A report appearing in the Czechoslovak press in spring 1972 on expected economic developments during the next five years prompted an identical question by RFE to its respondents (RFE, 1973a), which found that the latter were far more pessimistic than those interviewed at home.

Extensive polling during the Dubček era (reported in Piekalkiewicz, 1972) provides yet another opportunity to validate RFE surveys. Contrasting the set conducted between August 1965 and January 1967 on recent changes in living standards (RFE, 1967a) with a Czechoslovak survey of December 1968 again shows greater pessimism among RFE's visitors to the West. Similarly, although enthusiasm for the reforms and Dubček himself prior to the Soviet intervention was almost identical in Czechoslovak and RFE polls, as reported by the latter (RFE, 1968b; 1968c), in less euphoric times differences were far more striking. Dubček's popularity dropped off sharply after August 1968 among RFE respondents (RFE, 1968a; 1969), but remained at high albeit declining levels among those interviewed in Czechoslovak polls. In mid-1968, offered a choice in free elections, about seven in eight of those interviewed by RFE and making a choice opted for "bourgeois" parties (RFE, 1973b); in indigenous surveys, only 42 percent of all making a choice and 59 percent of the noncommunists would make the same decision, with the remainder casting ballots for the Czechoslovak Communist Party. More generally, in contrast to the high degree of acceptance in 1968 of the socialist system, as reported earlier, an RFE survey in 1967 found practically no respondents whose basic attitude on the idea *and* practice of communism was one of acceptance, and almost half who rejected it (RFE, 1967a).

Uses of Data from Closed Societies

The confrontation of these two different kinds of data points to one of the key aspects of all such data. Variations in results may well stem from the wording of questions, events intervening between one survey and the next, or especially differences in samples. RFE and Czechoslovak surveys may *both* be accurate reflections of a multifaceted reality. To look at either as being the whole and exclusive truth would surely be misleading, but then, so too would be their rejection out of hand by analysts as being wholly inaccurate. A study using such data must concern itself seriously with their context.

A second point, implicit in the first, is that such data confrontations permit analysts to get a better idea of just what aspect of the social reality any particular set of data taps. If we know that, compared to their countrymen, RFE respondents pay somewhat (but not much) more attention to the media, are generally more conservative, and usually respond more quickly to changes in political events, then we have a better basis to evaluate RFE data for which no validation studies exist. In this sense, substantial changes in the views of RFE respondents, in whatever direction, may presage equally important changes in the structure of public opinion in their home country.

Third, if technical aspects of any particular kind of survey remain the same over time, then the data produced by a series of such surveys can be valuable in a relative sense even if they are off the mark in absolute terms. Let us assume, for instance, that indigenous Czechoslovak surveys in fact accurately indicate how the mass public would vote in the event of a free election and that RFE surveys yield data substantially at variance. Changes in the latter over time will nonetheless provide indicators of *trends* of opinion. If we were to detect a significant change in them—toward or away from the local communist party, perhaps, or indeed changes in the expressed willingness of people to vote in such an hypothetical election (RFE, 1973b)—then we might reasonably conclude that similar changes, albeit not of a similar magnitude or at the same level, are occurring in the population at large.

Finally, as is true of public opinion surveying in general, the results seem to be more valid the closer the questions get to the respondents' day-to-day behavior—that is, communists and noncommunists alike, and stay-at-homes as well as foreign travelers, pay about the same amount of attention to the media—and the more critical variables in explaining differences among groups are levels of education, socioeconomic status, and the like. When we turn to touchy political issues, on which respondents might for reasons of personal security or national pride want to hedge, we find the greatest amount of variance. This finding is certainly one among other reasons why HICOG surveyers focused their interviews with GDR citizens ever more on the practical issues of how they liked American exhibits at the industrial and agricultural fairs, what radio stations they listened to, and what themes stressed by American propaganda seemed best to capture their attention.

The point is not that we can ignore technical problems, particularly that of the representativeness of the sample, in evaluating efforts to get systematic data on popular perspectives in closed societies. We cannot. Rather, by taking into account the advantages and limitations offered by the technical procedures, we can better use the data for analysis. Estimating margins of error, looking at changes and trends, and recognizing that differences in validity stem also from the substantive area on which questions are asked are first steps in this direction.

References

Ahlberg, René. 1969. "Theorie der öffentlichen Meinung und empirische Meinungsforschung in der UdSSR." *Osteuropa 19:3 (March):161-72.*

Almond, Gabriel A. 1950. *The American People and Foreign Policy.* New York: Harcourt (republished in 1960; New York: Praeger).

Bauer, Raymond A., Alex Inkeles, and Clyde Kluckhohn. 1957. *How the Soviet System Works: Cultural, Psychological, and Social Themes.* Cambridge: Harvard University Press.

Benedict, Ruth. 1946. *The Chrysanthemum and the Sword: Patterns of Japanese Culture.* Boston: Houghton Mifflin.

Boberach, Heinz, ed. 1965. *Meldungen aus dem Reich: Auswahl aus den geheimen Lageberichten des Sicherheitsdienstes der SS 1939-1944.* Neuwied and Berlin: Luchterhand.

Cohen, Bernard C. 1973. *The Public's Impact on Foreign Policy.* Boston: Little, Brown.

Dicks, Henry V. 1972. *Licensed Mass Murder: A Socio-Psychological Study of Some SS Killers.* New York: Basic Books.

——. 1952. "Observations on Contemporary Russian Behavior." *Human Relations* 5:2 (May):111-75.

Geiger, H. Kent. 1968. *The Family in Soviet Russia.* Cambridge: Harvard University Press.

George, Alexander L. 1959. *Propaganda Analysis: A Study of Inferences Made from Nazi Propaganda in World War II.* White Plains: Row, Peterson.

Gleitman, Henry and Joseph J. Greenbaum. 1960. "Hungarian Socio-Political Attitudes and Revolutionary Action." *Public Opinion Quarterly* 24:1 (Spring):62-76.

Gorer, Geoffrey and John Rickman. 1949. *The People of Great Russia: A Psychological Study.* London: Cresset.

Gurfein, Murray I. and Morris Janowitz. 1946. "Trends in Wehrmacht Morale." *Public Opinion Quarterly* 10:1 (Spring):78-84.

Halpern, Henry. 1949. "Soviet Attitude toward Public Opinion Research in Germany." *Public Opinion Quarterly* 13:1 (Spring):117-18.

Inkeles, Alex and Raymond A. Bauer. 1959. *The Soviet Citizen: Daily Life in a Totalitarian Society.* Cambridge: Harvard University Press.

International Public Opinion Research (IPOR). 1953. *Media of Communication and the Free World as Seen by Czechoslovak, Hungarian, and Polish Refugees: Comparative Report.* New York: International Public Opinion Research, Inc.

International Studies of Values in Politics. 1971. *Values and the Active Community: A Cross-National Study of the Influence of Local Leadership*. New York: Free Press.

Kracauer, Siegfried and Paul L. Berkman. 1956. *Satellite Mentality: Political Attitudes and Propaganda Susceptibilities of Non-Communists in Hungary, Poland and Czechoslovakia*. New York: Praeger.

Lasswell, Harold D. 1927. *Propaganda Technique in the World War*. New York: Knopf (republished in 1971; Cambridge: M.I.T. Press).

Lerner, Daniel. 1949. *Sykewar: Psychological Warfare against Germany, D-Day to VE-Day*. New York: Stewart (republished in 1971; Cambridge: M.I.T. Press).

Levy, David M. 1947. *New Fields of Psychiatry*. New York: Norton.

Mead, Margaret. 1951. *Soviet Attitudes toward Authority: An Interdisciplinary Approach to Problems of Soviet Character*. New York: McGraw-Hill.

Merritt, Anna J. and Richard L. Merritt. 1970. *Public Opinion in Occupied Germany: The OMGUS Surveys, 1945-1949*. Urbana: University of Illinois Press.

_____ and _____ . Forthcoming. *Public Opinion in Semisovereign Germany: The HICOG Surveys, 1949-1955*. Urbana: University of Illinois Press.

Mink, Georges. 1975. "Concept et sondage d'opinion publique en Union Soviétique." *Revue de l'Est* 6:1 (March): 207-18.

Noelle, Elisabeth. 1940. *Amerikanische Massenbefraugungen über Politik und Presse*. Frankfurt/Main: Diesterweg.

Paulu, Burton. 1974. *Radio and Television Broadcasting in Eastern Europe*. Minneapolis: University of Minnesota Press.

Pethybridge, Roger. 1967. "The Assessment of Ideological Influences on East Europeans." *Public Opinion Quarterly* 31:1 (Spring):38-50.

Piekalkiewicz, Jaroslaw A. 1972. *Public Opinion Polling in Czechoslovakia, 1968-69: Results and Analysis of Surveys Conducted during the Dubček Era*. New York: Praeger.

Pozner, Vladimir, Juri Filinovich, and Yuri Sherapov. 1965. "Soviet Youth Answer Gallup Poll Questions." *Soviet Life* 11/110 (November):7-14.

Radio Free Europe, Audience and Public Opinion Research Department. 1967a. *Certain Key Political Attitudes and Economic Concerns in Czechoslovakia*. Munich: RFE (February).

_____. 1967b. *Newspaper Readership in Poland in the Light of RFE Findings and Findings of the Polish Radio Research Center*. Munich: RFE (April).

117

_____. 1968a. *The Crisis of Confidence among Czechs and Slovaks*. Munich: RFE (December).

_____. 1968b. *The Height of Dubček's Popularity*. Munich: RFE (September).

_____. 1968c. *Popular Support of Dubček and the Action Program in Czechoslovakia*. Munich: RFE (August).

_____. 1969. *Czechoslovakia 1969: The Crisis of Confidence*. Munich: RFE (December).

_____. 1971. *Polish Expectations about War and Opinions about the Influence of Key Mass Media in the Mirror of Internal and APOR Polls*. Munich: RFE (October).

_____. 1972a. *Czechoslovak Attitudes to War in the Light of Internal and External Surveys*. Munich: RFE (October).

_____. 1972b. *Domestic Poll Results on Listening to Radio Warsaw*. Munich: RFE (April).

_____. 1972c. *Some Aspects of Exposure to the Press and Radio as Measured inside Poland and by APOR-RFE*. Munich: RFE (September).

_____. 1973a. *Economic Expectations in Czechoslovakia*. Munich: RFE (December).

_____. 1973b. *Hypothetical Free Elections in East Europe (1968-1972)*. Munich: RFE (March).

Schröter, Gerhard. 1958. *Jugendliche Flüchtlinge aus der Sowjetzone*. Munich: Infratest.

Sheldon, Richard C. and John Dutkowski. 1952-53. "Are Soviet Satellite Refugee Interviews Projectable?" *Public Opinion Quarterly* 16:4 (Winter):579-94.

Shils, Edward A. and Morris Janowitz. 1948. "Cohesion and Disintegration in the Wehrmacht in World War II." *Public Opinion Quarterly* 12:2 (Summer):280-315.

Solomon, Richard H. 1971. *Mao's Revolution and the Chinese Political Culture*. Berkeley: University of California Press.

Szalai, Alexander, ed. 1972. *The Use of Time: Daily Activities of Urban and Suburban Populations in Twelve Countries*. The Hague: Mouton.

White, Stephen. 1973. "Communist Political Culture: An Empirical Note." *Newsletter on Comparative Studies of Communism* 6:2 (February):41-44.

13

What Decision Units Shape Foreign Policy: Individual, Group, Bureaucracy?

Charles F. Hermann

Contending Perspectives

The surge in literature on bureaucratic politics has accelerated consideration of the role of governmental structures and processes in foreign policy. One such approach studies bureaucratic organizations (decision unit structures) and their processes (bureaucratic politics) to explain how organizational arrangements affect foreign policy outputs (e.g., Halperin, 1974; Hilsman, 1967; Neustadt, 1960). Policymakers, the bureaucratic perspective contends, normally work in the context of large and often competing bureaucratic organizations. With their outlook on international affairs shaped by their department or agency, these individuals struggle to establish policies that will protect, if not advance, the basic interests of their governmental unit. Thus, the "resultant [or content of policy] is not chosen as a solution to a problem but rather results from compromise, conflict, and confusion of officials with diverse interests and unequal influence" (Allison, 1971, p. 162). The advocates of the bureaucratic politics perspective assert that the process by which policy is made is not neutral, but has a profound impact on the resultant. A question of extreme importance if such insights are to be useful is, When, or under what conditions, will the bureaucratic players be a decisive force?

Other studies have underscored the impact of small group processes (e.g., Verba, 1961; de Rivera, 1968; Paige, 1968; Byars, 1973). For example, the psychologist Irving Janis (1972, p. 9) suggests that some major failures in American foreign policy decisions resulted from excessive concurrence-seeking among members of small, cohesive policy groups. Their decision process led to a "deterioration of mental efficiency, reality testing, and moral judgment." In contrast to the conflict and bargaining of bureaucratic politics, then, Janis attributes powerful effects to strongly shared norms and cohesion among the participants.

Still another perspective is introduced by investigators who study the policy process from the level of individual policymakers (e.g., George, 1969; Stassen, 1972; Hermann, 1974). In this view, policy depends upon individual characteristics such as operational codes, personality traits, or modes of conducting interpersonal relationships. As Barber (1972, p. 6) declares, "a President's personality is an important shaper of his Presidential behavior on non-trivial matters." In sum, a decision may be the manifestation of the personal characteristics of a key decisionmaker who is little affected by either the pulling and hauling of bureaucratic politics or the pressure of a small group to conform to its norms.[a]

These brief references to the effects on foreign policy of bureaucratic politics, small group dynamics, and personal characteristics reveal potential conflict among the alternative kinds of explanations they employ. Although simplified here and hence exaggerating somewhat differences in their explanatory mechanism, each contributes variously in explaining foreign policy:[b] (1) any given perspective might not contribute importantly in accounting for behavior under any identifiable conditions; (2) the perspective might interact with one or more other elements that in combination produce a distinctive impact on behavior; and (3) the perspective might have a direct and important effect under specified conditions. The balance of this chapter briefly explores the third possibility.

Limiting Conditions

Each perspective identifies a decision unit employing a more or less distinctive process. Bureaucratic politics involves participants from independent governmental organizations having autonomous goals. The participants adhere to their organizations' goals and seek to further them. Action results from political bargaining and maneuvering among the bureaucratic players. Small group decisionmaking (of which "groupthink" is but one possible consequence) involves a set of individuals who interact—frequently face-to-face—and who share norms about appropriate group behavior. All members attach high value to the group and its abilities to perform decision tasks. Action results from group deliberation procedures that minimize lasting disharmony in the group. Finally, individual choices reflect the preferences of a single person regardless of whether or not the decisions are ratified by some collectivity. Action results from efforts of the individual to fulfill his basic motives, values, beliefs, attitudes, and modes of cognition.

Two basic conditioning variables may differentiate the circumstances in

---

[a] Janis (1972, p. 196) also notes that leadership personality may be an alternative explanation for behaviors he attributes to "groupthink," and proposes future research on internalized group norms versus convergence on the leader's actual or putative desires.

[b] Of course, many other elements have been either hypothesized or shown to influence certain types of foreign policy behavior. Much of the work on these three perspectives has focused almost exclusively on American policy. Serious challenges can be raised about their relative adequacy for other nations, requiring consideration of the impact of political régime differences, national attributes, and so on. In this essay, however, attention is restricted to alternative decision units operating within governments.

which these alternative decision units emerge. They are the nature of the situation and the stages of policy. By *situation* is meant the transitory elements of a government's environment associated with the occasion for decision. Elsewhere (Hermann, 1969, 1972; Brady, 1973) various specific situational properties have been described and their implications examined, but in this discussion they will be collapsed into crisis and noncrisis.[c] In a crisis, the threat to major governmental goals results in the increased likelihood that high-level policymakers will become involved. Furthermore, the limited time for a decision in crisis and the importance of secrecy act to limit the overall number of participants. These characteristics predispose the decision process—with some important qualifications to be noted below—toward either small group or individual decision units. By contrast, in noncrisis situations, more people are likely to become involved but without officials from the highest levels of government. Other things being equal, these features of a noncrisis tend to increase the participation of representatives from multiple bureaucratic organizations. High-level participation tends to minimize bureaucratic politics because such policymakers are less likely to identify their future careers with the well-being of one particular bureaucracy and are more likely to feel a direct, personal responsibility to the head of state who often can directly affect their tenure in office and/or the authority they exercise. When the time available for handling a policy issue is not constrained (as it is in a crisis), more bureaus have time for appraising the situation in terms of their own interests and their expressions of desire to participate in the decision process can less readily be disregarded.

The *stages of policy* comprise a conditioning variable that refers to the sequence of activities that are involved in treating a policy problem. Various ways of classifying the decision process have been advanced but for this essay a simplified three-stage distinction will be used. First, there is the *problem identification and elaboration* phase in which various intelligence and analysis activities play a central role. In societies with large and complex governmental structures, this stage normally involves bureaucratic organizations regardless of the situation. The second stage involves the activities associated with the actual *decision* or choice. It includes the enumeration and evaluation of alternatives as well as the selection of one. *Implementation*, as a third stage, involves those activities judged to be appropriate to carry out the preferred option. Different kinds of decision units can, and often are, involved in different stages of policy.

To evaluate more clearly the impact of the last two stages on the probable decision unit, an additional variable needs to be considered with

---

[c] Crisis situations are those involving a high threat to goals of the government, short decision time, and surprise to the policymakers (Hermann, 1969). Here noncrisis is a residual category of all other situations.

reference to each phase. During the actual selection of an alternative (decision stage), it is important to establish how power is distributed among the participants. If there is an hierarchy in which one individual is dominant and all others are subordinate to him, then the individual decision unit tends to be dominant in both crisis and noncrisis situations. On the other hand, if there is a rough equality in the power of those participating in the choice selection (i.e., no person is in a position to dictate his choice regardless of the preferences of all the others), then the probable decision unit will be different in crisis than in noncrisis. In a crisis, the small number of high-level policymakers leads naturally to the small-group form of decision-making. For a noncrisis, the participants may meet in groups, but they will be representatives of different bureaucratic organizations. Bureaucratic politics will prevail.

Once a decision is reached, energy is directed to implementation. Some policies require verbal actions only whereas others entail physical resource allocation. The physical resources include both human and nonhuman resources and their utilization in foreign policy in any but the most minimal way involves considerable coordination, communication, and control. In brief, it requires the supervision of complex organizations. Because such assignments seldom appear neutral to the well-being of governmental agencies, they trigger bureaucratic politics to either obtain, avoid, or reinterpret the directive. In crises where political leaders recognize that the stakes are high for themselves and their régimes, efforts to control and limit bureaucratic initiatives contrary to the wishes of those who made the decision occur with more or less success. Without a crisis, however, the constraints on bureaucratic politics in the implementation of a decision are minimal.

Precisely because the decisionmakers in a crisis recognize the importance of maintaining control over the execution of their decisions, delegation of actions requiring only verbal behavior is either nonexistent or restricted to trusted associates. The speech, negotiation, or message in a crisis is normally the product of one individual or a small group.

The variables considered in this chapter do not give a clear picture of the probable decision unit responsible for implementing a verbal decision in a noncrisis. A general assumption has been that the attributes of a cohesive group are less likely to emerge when the participants are middle-level officials whose careers are based in different organizations. This assertion appears to stress interaction among bureaucratic organizations. But, if the stakes for any bureau, agency, or organization are low (little threat), then the possibility of a determined individual affixing his imprimatur on implementation increases. Similarly, if a small, cohesive group exists, then it too could take over the execution of a decision.

References

Allison, Graham T. 1971. *Essence of Decision: Explaining the Cuban Missile Crisis*. Boston: Little, Brown.

Barber, James David. 1972. *The Presidential Character: Predicting Performance in the White House*. Englewood Cliffs: Prentice-Hall.

Brady, Linda P. 1974. "Threat, Decision Time, and Awareness." Ph.D. dissertation. Columbus: The Ohio State University.

Byars, Robert S. 1973. "Small-Group Theory and Shifting Styles of Political Leadership." *Comparative Political Studies* 5:1 (January):443-69.

De Rivera, Joseph H. 1968. *The Psychological Dimension of Foreign Policy*. Columbus: Charles Merrill.

George, Alexander L. 1969. "The 'Operational Code': A Neglected Approach to the Study of Political Leaders and Decision-Making." *International Studies Quarterly* 13:2 (June):190-222.

Halperin, Morton H. 1974. *Bureaucratic Politics and Foreign Policy*. Washington: The Brookings Institution.

Hermann, Charles F. 1969. "Crisis as a Situational Variable," pp. 409-21, in James N. Rosenau, ed., *International Politics and Foreign Policy*. New York: Free Press (rev. ed.).

_____, ed. 1972. *International Crises*. New York: Free Press.

Hermann, Margaret G. 1974. "Leader Personality and Foreign Policy Behavior," in James N. Rosenau, ed. *Comparing Foreign Policy*. Beverly Hills: Sage.

Hilsman, Roger. 1967. *To Move a Nation: The Politics of Foreign Policy in the Administration of John F. Kennedy*. New York: Doubleday.

Janis, Irving L. 1972. *Victims of Groupthink: A Psychological Study of Foreign Policy Decisions*. Boston: Houghton Mifflin.

Neustadt, Richard E. 1960. *Presidential Power: The Politics of Leadership*. New York: Wiley.

Paige, Glenn D. 1968. *The Korean Decision, June 24-30, 1950*. New York: Free Press.

Stassen, Glen H. 1972. "Individual Preferences versus Role-Constraints in Policy-Making: Senatorial Response to Secretaries Acheson and Dulles." *World Politics* 25:1 (October):96-119.

Verba, Sidney. 1961. *Small Groups and Political Behavior*. Princeton, N.J.: Princeton University Press.

14 The Military and Foreign Policy: The Role of the Joint Chiefs of Staff

Lawrence J. Korb

The principal military input into the foreign policy process normally comes from the four-man Joint Chiefs of Staff (JCS). This chapter analyzes the role of the JCS in this process by discussing three interrelated areas: (1) the sources of the Chiefs' foreign policy preferences; (2) the manner in which these preferences are conveyed to the key decisionmakers; and (3) the impact of the JCS upon foreign policy. Most of the data for this analysis comes from interviews conducted with thirteen retired Chiefs in the period from 1968 through 1974.

Sources

The foreign policy positions of the members of the JCS are primarily the result of a desire to protect and enhance the interests and essence of their own services. During the post-SALT II debates over future U.S. strategic policy, the Chief of Naval Operations (CNO), Admiral Elmo R. Zumwalt, argued that the ICBM was becoming obsolete and that this nation ought to rely for deterrence on the Navy's SLBM. Air Force Chief of Staff, General George S. Brown, countered with the proposition that his studies demonstrated that the Air Force's ICBM would be invulnerable through 1990. Since the interests of three military services are often not identical, the JCS sometimes deliver split opinions. However, when the Chiefs see that their splits will be capitalized upon by civilian officials, they usually compromise their differences and present a united military front to the civilian policymakers. During the 1960s, the JCS unanimously agreed that this nation needed a new manned bomber for the Air Force, nuclear-powered aircraft carriers for the Navy, and an ABM for the Army even though some of the Chiefs had strong reservations about each of these systems. The JCS did this because they knew that Secretary of Defense Robert S. McNamara was opposed to all three programs and would attempt to use dissent among the JCS to legitimize his own opinion.

When one looks at the backgrounds and responsibilities of the JCS, it is not surprising that service interests are the source of their policy preferences. Since the establishment of the JCS in 1947, thirty men have been appointed to it. The average age of these officers at the time of their appointment was 54 with an average of 33 years of commissioned service. Only two men have ever been selected to the JCS before reaching their 50th birthday or with less than 30 years of service. Ninety percent of the Chiefs have been graduates of either West Point or Annapolis at a time when these academies offered only a single-track, technical curriculum almost devoid of socio-humanistic courses. Only one of these officers had an post-graduate training outside of the military's own professional, staff, or War Colleges. All of the Chiefs have been combat-oriented line officers whose main accomplishment was demonstrated expertise in the weapons systems peculiar to their own services. Few of these men had any significant or extensive staff, joint, or nonmilitary experience. Finally, the advancement of all of these officers to the top ten positions in their services, from which the president usually chooses his Chiefs, is rigidly controlled by the services.

As a result of their 30 to 40 years of association with their service, most members of the JCS are unable or unwilling to rise above service particularism. All of the Chiefs, except the chairman, wear two hats. In addition to being the principal military advisers to the policymakers, they are also the military heads of their own services, which they perceive as their primary role. In spite of a 1958 law that specifically directs them to give priority to their joint function, the service Chiefs devote most of their time and energy to running their own services. Admiral Arthur W. Radford, the only man to be selected for chairman without having first served as service chief, was bitterly disappointed and spent much of his time as chairman trying to run the Navy. Moreover, each time that a suggestion is made that the JCS formally divest themselves of their service responsibilities, the Chiefs resist it strongly.

Even if an individual officer were capable and desirous of rising above his service background when he reached the JCS, the political realities of his position make it nearly impossible to do so. Before each JCS meeting, service chiefs are traditionally briefed by their own service staffs rather than the Joint Staff. Members of the service view their military head as their "chief lobbyist" and look with great disapproval on any of his actions that might undermine their service position. When Admiral Louis E. Denfeld, CNO from 1947 to 1949, accepted the decision of Secretary of Defense Louis Johnson to cancel a supercarrier, his admirals "revolted" and took the Navy's case to the public and the Congress, without Denfeld's permission, and Harry Truman fired Denfeld for losing control of his service (Hammond, 1963, p. 546).

The chairman of the JCS, with no service responsibilities, is expected to rise above the parochialism of his service. However, members of his service still look to the chairman to represent their views and he usually does. Military leaders, recognizing this, have urged that the chairmanship be rotated among the three services. When Maxwell Taylor broke the rotation pattern by coming out of retirement in 1962 to succeed another Army general as chairman, he incurred the wrath of officers of all the services. It is more than coincidence that the Navy emerged with the largest share of the defense budget during the Nixon Administration when Admiral Thomas H. Moorer was chairman. Likewise, the Army prospered during the Kennedy and Johnson years when Army Generals Maxwell D. Taylor and Earle G. Wheeler served as chairmen, while it received the smallest part of the defense budget during the Eisenhower years when the Navy and Air Force controlled the top spot.

Access

Because the 1947 National Security Act and its subsequent amendments make the JCS the principal military advisers to the president, the Secretary of Defense, and the Congress, a number of formalized channels of access for the JCS have become institutionalized. JCS input to the president comes primarily through the National Security Council (NSC) system. The chairman is a statutory adviser to the Council and a member of its major subcommittees. In addition the chief executive allows the JCS an annual "day in court" to discuss the upcoming defense budget. JCS opinions are made known to the Secretary of Defense in two ways. The secretary usually attends one of the tri-weekly JCS meetings, and each year the JCS send thousands of written position papers to the defense chief on various national security issues. The Chiefs give their advice to the Congress in their annual committee appearances.

In addition to these formalized channels of access, a number of informal means are used by the JCS to present their viewpoints. Earle Wheeler attended the Tuesday lunches of Lyndon Johnson, and Thomas Moorer was usually present at Henry Kissinger's Friday breakfasts. The Chiefs often use their extensive contacts with Congress to plant questions and leak selected information (e.g., Admiral Radford let it be known publicly that he favored American involvement in Indochina in 1954 [Halperin, 1974, pp. 183-84]). Finally, the JCS can make use of the 39,000 military personnel serving with other government agencies to convey their positions. In 1971, Secretary of the Treasury George P. Shultz persuaded Secretary of Defense Melvin R. Laird to accept a $2 billion reduction in the FY 1972 budget. The Chiefs used their liaison officers on Henry Kissinger's staff to make known their unhappiness, and Kissinger convinced Nixon to over-rule Shultz and Laird.

Impact

Despite their multifaceted means of access, the overall impact of the JCS on post-World War II foreign policy has been minimal. The Chiefs have been so preoccupied with protecting their own interests that they never have been the source of any of the major doctrines that have shaped this nation's relations with the world. Policies such as containment, massive retaliation, flexible response, Vietnamization, and détente have been developed with negligible input from the JCS. Many times the JCS were not consulted during the formulation process, but even when they were asked to contribute, they usually refused. The Chiefs declined to participate in the drafting of NSC-68, which formed the basis for containment (Schilling, Hammond, and Snyder, 1962, p. 296).

The Chiefs' main function has been to legitimize and occasionally modify proposals developed elsewhere in the bureaucracy. Because of the Chiefs' status as military experts and because of their easy access to Congress and the public, political leaders have felt it necessary to get the Chiefs ''on board'' before undertaking any new foreign policy initiatives. On some occasions, the JCS have been able to modify certain policies in return for their approval. The JCS agreed to support the nuclear test ban treaty of 1963 only if it included a provision that would allow underground testing (Taylor, 1972, pp. 282-87). Likewise, JCS support for SALT I was made contingent upon administration support for several new weapons systems. The Chiefs' greatest ability to modify policies comes during wartime. When the shooting starts, even powerful civilian officials like Secretary of Defense McNamara are reluctant to challenge the military professionals. Thus, during the Vietnamese conflict the JCS were able to persuade the Johnson administration to increase bombing levels and troop strength beyond their planned levels (Sheehan et al., 1971). The Chiefs also coupled their support for Johnson's war policies to his support for the ABM (Hoopes, 1969, p. 90). Similarly, the Nixon Chiefs supported Vietnamization in return for permission to attack Viet Cong sanctuaries in Cambodia.

However, on many occasions the Chiefs have publicly supported policies to which they were opposed and which they were unable to modify. In the pre-Korean War period the JCS supported President Truman's meager defense budgets before a skeptical Congress (Schilling, Hammond, and Snyder, 1962, pp. 54-94). Likewise, the Chiefs refused to tell Congress about their objections to Eisenhower's ''new look'' defense policies (Kolodziej, 1966, pp. 203-14).

Conclusion

The JCS were created as a compromise between those who wanted unification of the armed services and those who desired to keep them separate. Torn between both camps, and staffed by men who are a product of a 40-year narrow socialization process, the Chiefs have rarely been a source of innovation in the foreign policy process. However, because of their access to both the executive and legislative branches and their status as military experts, they have been able to modify many policies, especially during wartime.

References

Halperin, Morton H. 1974. *Bureaucratic Politics and Foreign Policy*. Washington: The Brookings Institution.

Hammond, Paul Y. 1963. "Supercarriers and B-36 Bombers," pp. 465-564, in Harold Stein, ed., *American Civil-Military Decisions: A Book of Case Studies*. University of Alabama Press.

Hoopes, Townsend. 1969. *The Limits of Intervention: The Inside Account of How the Johnson Policy of Escalation in Vietnam was Reversed*. New York: McKay.

Kolodziej, Edward A. 1966. *The Uncommon Defense and Congress, 1945-1963*. Columbus: Ohio State University Press.

Korb, Lawrence J. 1976. *The Joint Chiefs of Staff: The First Twenty-Five Years*. Bloomington: Indiana University Press.

Schilling, Warner R., Paul Y. Hammond, and Glenn H. Snyder. 1962. *Strategy, Politics, and Defense Budgets*. New York: Columbia University Press.

Sheehan, Neil, Hedrick Smith, E. W. Kenworthy, and Fox Butterfield. 1971. *The Pentagon Papers*. New York: Bantam.

Taylor, Maxwell D. 1972. *Swords and Plowshares*. New York: Norton.

Part V
Policies for National Security

15 National Security Policy Formation in Comparative Perspective

Ernst W. Gohlert

The problem faced by the analyst of national security affairs is twofold. First, what are the essential security phenomena? Second, how are we to determine key variables and, once established, how should they be analyzed? Satisfactory responses to these difficult yet rudimentary questions are still lacking. In view of the essentially historical, episodic, and fragmentary nature of the literature on national security (cf. Rosser, 1974, p. vii; Singer, 1961, pp. 83-84), it is not surprising that operational concepts, hypotheses, generalizations, and theories are in short supply. Nonetheless, the scientific study of security data is possible.

Assumptions

Two sets of assumptions are particularly relevant. First, it is assumed that security phenomena are closely related to vital interests (Morgenthau, 1951); that security is generally understood in military terms instead of international cooperation, negotiation, or compromise (Rudoy, 1972); but that security is not the equivalent of power (Wolfers, 1952, pp. 484-86).

A second set of assumptions maintains that a qualitative difference exists between national security data in particular and foreign policy phenomena in general (cf. Rosenau, 1971, p. 67ff.; Singer, 1961, p. 91). In short, national security policy refers to a distinct arena of policy with a high priority rating. Further, because of their select status—but this is not the only reason—security data are treated as a legitimate subject of inquiry within the larger context of domestic and international politics. Finally, it is assumed that laboratory conditions for these complex political data can be approximated only through reliance on the comparative method. In other words, the pertinence of variables and the validity of generalizations cannot be tested except against data from different political systems, national and international (Horton, 1974b, p. ix).

Boundaries

Previous theory-conscious research (e.g., Wolfers, 1952; Rosenau, 1971) viewed security as both an instrumental objective and a specific field. The crucial question is, security of or for what? As a goal, security means the protection of core values. According to Wolfers (1952, pp. 484-85), security protects "values previously acquired" and in its objective and subjective sense, respectively, measures "the absence of threats to acquired values" and "the absence of fear that such values will be attacked." The nature and scope of these values is the product of individual and collective judgment. Although difficult, it is not impossible to subject the normative character of security to empirical analysis. It involves three steps: specification of (1) core values, (2) the level of security sought, and (3) the corresponding means (cf. Wolfers, 1952). Core values are not fixed. They are subject to constant variation in every respect. They may include such broad goals as survival, territorial integrity, political and economic independence as well as cultural and ideological considerations. In praxis, these steps require a study of security elites and their bureaucratic apparatus, the processes of socialization, and the dominant value systems. It calls also for an investigation of the costs individual and organizational actors are prepared to incur in their pursuit of a particular level of security. Finally, it is necessary to test the scope of security concerns by probing the means (e.g., military preparedness, diplomatic moves, reliance on international organizations, and so forth), which in fact correspond to security policies.

This perspective of the essential aspects of security is consequential for the boundaries of security as a field. Due to the fact that the normative content of security is variable, no definitive empirical boundaries can be established. Analytically, the boundaries of the security arena coincide with the delineation of core values, the level of protection (what price security?), and the means for protection. Therefore, the distinction between security and foreign policy data turns on these criteria. The lack of analytic precision—for example, in the distinction between core and secondary values—is not fatal, because it is compensated for in part by the laboratory conditions of comparative analysis, which permit a general perspective. The decisive point is whether heuristic categories for comparative security analysis have been provided.

In order to sharpen the focus on the essential features of security, it is useful to consider Rosenau's (1971, p. 214) notion of "calculated control," which he defines as "the calculated acts and the processes of interaction whereby behavior is modified across national boundaries." Such acts can be observed and measured roughly in terms of the behavior of controllers and controllees, their decisions, interactions, control capacities, their control techniques, control limits, targets, and so forth. The corresponding policies are generically referred to as "undertakings." In summary, we may now define security policy as *efforts at calculated control expressed in specific undertakings with the implicit or explicit goal to promote an environment favorable to the protection of values previously acquired.*

Variables and Propositions

One major task for analysts is to gather data and search for variables with the aim of developing a security index for purposes of measuring security phenomena and testing hypotheses and generalizations. These steps are essential for the development of a general body of knowledge.

Following Rosenau's lead in the comparative foreign policy field, the security index suggested below derives in part from empirical research on security affairs and from my own comparative work (Gohlert, 1974). The criteria for selecting security variables stem from empirical and intellectual considerations. For example, the concern for useful categorization of data is matched by the equally important need to formulate generalizations. The index structure corresponds to the preceding conception of security and its boundaries. It consists of the following four independent and/or dependent variables:

1. Individual Actors—socialization, values, conceptions, roles;
2. Organizational Actors—values, roles, formal and informal organizational structures/bureaucratic politics;
3. Domestic Environment—political culture, human and nonhuman resources;
4. External Environment—power configurations, interactions, communication/feedback loops.

In applied form, the values and roles (variables 1 and 2) and the specific constraints of the environments (variables 3 and 4) serve as indicators of the nature and scope of security concerns. The potency of each variable vis-à-vis security policy is a function of variance within each cluster as well as between all factors comprising the index. Furthermore, it should not be presumed that the present security index is definitive or that the categories are mutually exclusive. This important although unfortunate qualification is indicative of the present state of research and theory in the study of national security policy formation.

Despite this qualification, the test of significance and validity, and the question of quality with respect to the resulting propositions, cannot be avoided. It is therefore necessary to point to some yardsticks. For example, data relevant to East-West détente, with specific reference to the United States and West Germany, analyzed from the perspective of the security index, permit a measure of its worth. First, it makes possible a meaningful differentiation of security concerns between superpowers and middle states. The difference lies in the respective variance of ends, means, and roles adhered to by the actors (variables 1 and 2) as well as the divergent constraints of the environments (variables 3 and 4). Specification of American and West German security needs and concerns in these categories contrasts with ambiguous and illusive distinctions simply in terms of interest and power.

Second, the index allows for a more specific evaluation of security data with respect to the impact of individual and organizational roles on policy. The evidence suggests, for instance, that the success of individual and organizational actors stands in a direct relationship to particular stages of policy development, which they attempt to manage and influence. Consequently, major policy innovations and breakthroughs (e.g., in West German *Ostpolitik* and American security policy toward China and the Soviet Union) are primarily the result of individual engagement. Similar conclusions apply to crisis management, whereas policy implementation and significant policy outcomes are more dependent on the capabilities of bureaucratic structures.

Finally, a list of propositions will indicate the level of generalization to which the approach may lead.

1. All political systems engage in acts of calculated control to prevent threats to acquired values.
2. Calculated control in the security area requires specialized modes of organization.
3. Security organization is a necessary, although not sufficient, condition for effective—that is, goal achieving—calculated control.
4. Whereas the propensity to organize for security corresponds approximately to the scope and intensity of security concerns, the ability to organize is circumscribed by limitations inherent in all variables, particularly the clusters comprising individual actors and domestic environment.
5. All things being equal, security organization is a measure of threat perception.
6. Calculated control with respect to security is operative in the external environment but success or failure tends to be determined within the domestic context.

The tentative nature of these propositions is evident, but merits some elaboration on interrelationships among variables. For example, if a security organization operates under conditions of extreme bureaucratization (variable 2), the significance—in terms of impact on the course of calculated control—of the domestic environment (variable 3) is heightened at the expense of individual actors (variable 1). In other words, as bureaucratic politics increases, internal battles among decisionmakers become as or more important than actual developments in the external environment, to the extent that no one individual or group of individuals is clearly in control. The situation remains unchanged until the process of deinstitutionalization has taken effect (cf. Ball, 1974).

Parallel to this hypothesis runs the following contention: If major actors (variable 2) become increasingly bureaucratized, then other actors (variable 4) will follow suit, in order to facilitate communication. The experience of West Germany and other middle states is illustrative of this.

As indicated by this discussion, comparative analysis of security policy formation is still in its infancy. With a good measure of optimism one may be tempted to conclude that we are perhaps approaching the pre-theory stage.

References

Ball, Desmond J. 1974. "The Blind Men and the Elephant: A Critique of Bureaucratic Politics Theory." *Australian Outlook* 28:1 (April): 71-92.

Gohlert, Ernst W. 1974. "An Organizational Perspective on German National Security Policy," pp. 146-55 in Horton (1974a).

Horton, Frank B., III, ed. 1974a. *Comparative Defense Policy*. Baltimore: Johns Hopkins University Press.

_____. 1974b. "Why Comparative Defense Policy?" pp. ix-x, in Horton (1974a).

Morgenthau, Hans J. 1951. *In Defense of the National Interest*. New York: Knopf.

Rosenau, James N. 1971. *The Scientific Study of Foreign Policy*. New York: Free Press.

Rosser, Richard F. 1974. "The Study of Comparative Defense Policy," pp. vii-viii, in Horton (1974a).

Rudoy, Dean William, ed. 1972. *In the Name of National Security*. Washington: Coalition on National Priorities and Military Policy.

Singer, J. David. 1961. "The Level-of-Analysis Problem in International Relations." *World Politics* 14:1 (October): 77-92.

Wolfers, Arnold. 1952. "'National Security' as an Ambiguous Symbol." *Political Science Quarterly* 67:1 (December): 481-502.

16 Technology Transfer and Détente

Ralph Sanders

Détente has significantly replaced the Cold War as the key relationship between the United States and the Soviet Union. Negotiations, not confrontation, have become their stated objective. Simultaneously, the world has developed a voracious appetite for advanced technology. In some technological areas, the United States enjoys a commanding position; in others, it imports from abroad. This discussion focuses on the decisionmaking process in the United States associated with the transfer of advanced technology to the Soviet Union under conditions of détente.

Technology transfer refers chiefly to the exchange or sale of three items: (1) products that result from technology; (2) the knowhow that undergirds technology; and (3) permission to manufacture patented products or patented licenses. Each type of transaction impacts differently on both the seller and buyer. This discussion is addressed largely to the exchange of technological knowhow related to commercial, rather than laboratory, activites and to knowhow that is extracted from items supplied.

First, a brief word about motivations. The United States promotes détente in the belief that improved relations with the Soviet Union afford the most effective means of preventing disastrous nuclear war. Among other things, providing the Soviets with technology seems to support this policy. The United States also hopes to gain as much economic benefit as it gives. Despite their continuing military buildup, the Soviets likewise say they want to avoid a nuclear holocaust. Moreover, the Soviet economy long has suffered from a lack of certain technological devices and skills. In fact, in fields like computers and computer applications to industrial production, in building large-bodied air transports, and in some oil and gas exploitation techniques, the United States remains the best, and sometimes the only, supplier. Soviet movement toward détente, in part, probably stems from a desire to gain access to these advanced technologies. The United States also could profitably import highly developed Soviet technologies like high voltage transmission.

Political and Legal Environment

The shift in political atmosphere has triggered a change in the statutory basis for East-West trade. During the Cold War, the United States aimed chiefly to deny the Soviets advanced technologies that could enhance their military capabilities. The Export Administration Act of 1969 shifted emphasis from denial to promotion of trade. Significant increases in contacts and commercial arrangements subsequently took place. Agreements signed in Moscow during 1972 and in Washington by President Richard Nixon and Chairman Leonid Brezhnev signaled a major acceleration in scientific cooperation. The most dramatic result was the bilateral Apollo-Soyuz Test Project under which each side designed its spacecraft to link up with the other in space in July 1975. Moreover, while prior to 1972 the U.S. share of Soviet imports of plant and equipment from the West was 5 percent, currently it totals some 20 percent.

The Decisionmaking Process

As is well known, policy questions in the United States largely are decided within a pluralistic decisionmaking system. Various actors, each with his own particular interests, often espouse conflicting views. The debate is centered in forums such as the bureaucracy, the business community, the general public, and, of course, in Congress and in the White House. Each protagonist's aim is to gain favorable legislation and presidential decisions. One way of gaining insight into the dynamics of this decisionmaking is to examine at least the chief actors, their motivations and arguments, and the interaction among them.

Department of State

Since the Secretary of State is the president's chief adviser on foreign policy as well as coordinator of all U.S. foreign relations, he plays an active role in questions of technology transfer to the Soviets. Intimately identified with détente, Secretary Henry Kissinger, in general, has supported increased exchanges. With the Departments of Defense and Commerce and the AEC, the State Department serves on an interagency working group that analyzes the broad implications of technology transfer and responds to questions from private industry.

Department of Commerce

The mission of the Department of Commerce is to support American business. Since it was set up to promote U.S. sales to communist countries, its Bureau of East-West Trade tends to adopt somewhat liberal attitudes toward granting technology transfers. Because this department has to approve or disapprove strategically significant exports to the U.S.S.R., it must consider national security aspects. Nonetheless, to the degree that technology transfer aids in promoting American business, the department tends to favor such transactions. Said one of its high officials (Tabor, 1974, p. 9), "I believe that agreements involving technology exchanges between the U.S.S.R. and either the U.S. Government or U.S. private companies can be quite beneficial to the U.S."

Department of Defense

Charged with protecting the nation, the Department of Defense takes a more cautious approach. Defense officials note the difficulty of distinguishing between technologies for peaceful trade and for war. They point out that in some cases the Soviets can divert acquired technology toward military ends. Moreover, by contributing to the Soviets' economic base, technology transfers ease their resource allocation problems and help them, if they wish, to maintain a high priority for military preparedness. The department views its role as advising on the military and national security aspects of these transactions. Besides being consulted on individual cases, defense officials are called on to present their views as to what items should appear on restricted lists. The department acknowledges that the United States can only delay, and not stop, the Soviets from attaining any military capability they pursue. Different perspectives between Defense and Commerce Department officials result in a more complete illumination of the transfer problem and a healthy airing of issues.

The Private Sector

The Soviets must acquire most of their needed technologies, not from governmental exchange programs, but from private U.S. firms. The American business community has reached no consensus as to how U.S. companies should respond and under what conditions. Some industrialists believe that centralized Soviet buyers can take advantage of fragmented, competing U.S. firms. They also fear that technology exports will build another competitor in foreign markets. Critics worry that the Soviets will buy only prototypes or production technology and then manufacture copies. For example, the strong competitive position of U.S. commercial air transport manufacturers might suffer. While these manufacturers disagree on the wisdom of providing the Soviets with the technological basis for a new aviation complex, all resist suggestions to export the latest technology for any joint design of new commercial aircraft.

Other industrialists contend that export sales can mean good business and that most technology that U.S. firms have to offer already is available in other Western countries. Some firms seem willing to export technologies a generation or so old. There is a belief in some business quarters that we can arrive at acceptable licensing and patent arrangements with the Soviets. The views of American businessmen coalesce and collide not only in the marketplace, but also in the advice they offer government officials and congressmen. In our pluralistic system, the opinions of businessmen (and other economic groups) find their way (as they should) into the councils that consider public issues.

International Bodies

The United States controls technology exports to the communist world in collaboration with an informal group comprising NATO countries and Japan. This Coordinating Committee on East-West Trade (COCOM) approves or denies exceptions to its list of embargoed items; decisions are unanimous and, while not binding, are rarely disregarded. West European countries long have sought trade with communist nations. COCOM's list, therefore, includes only prohibited items while the U.S. list is slightly longer. Over time, the number of embargoed items has declined as their strategic importance lessened although some advanced technologies were added.

Recent United States-Soviet agreements have triggered the creation of a spate of international organizations. At the top is the United States-U.S.S.R. Joint Commission on Scientific and Technical Cooperation, which has selected a number of broad areas for cooperation and fashioned policies to facilitate exchange of technical information. In contrast to COCOM, this and other bilateral bodies are charged with accelerating, rather than restricting, technology transfer. Their efforts affect intergovernmental arrangements more than commercial transactions involving U.S. companies. The advice they give to their home governments does affect technology transfer decisions.

Congress

Congress represents no unified public body. It should come as no surprise that congressmen differ on the wisdom of accelerating technology transfer to the Soviets. Some applaud the trend in the belief that such trade helps reinforce détente. Others are less sanguine. Congressman Ben Blackburn (R-Ga.) has argued that the Soviet military has benefited greatly from such transfers (U.S. Congress, 1974, H 934). Congress softened, but accepted an amendment offered by Senator Henry Jackson (D-Wash.) to a recent military procurement bill strengthening the Defense Department's hand in influencing such decisions. While insisting on adequate safeguards, Congress generally seems willing to permit the administration to explore ways of expanding technology exchanges with the Soviets.

The President

President Nixon's attitude toward technology transfer was conditioned by his advocacy of détente and President Gerald Ford, promising to continue this Nixon foreign policy, must consider two important questions. First, does the transfer support Soviet military development? Second, will it produce long-term advantages for the U.S. economy? It appears that the president is following the general policy that except where a clear danger to national security is demonstrated, technology transfer should be sympathetically considered.

The president does not take questions of national security lightly. The National Security Council (NSC) furnishes him with information and advice on issues of overall policy and on questions of sensitive export licensing clearances. In turn, the NSC receives recommendations from the Departments of State, Defense, Commerce, and other interested agencies as well as from the cabinet-level Council on International Economic Policy. The latter serves as a coordinating mechanism for all federal agencies concerned with foreign economic affairs. The president relies on this interdepartmental system to air all views and alternatives so that he can make balanced decisions.

For example, in 1970 President Nixon had to decide on a Soviet request to buy a British computer for use in a high energy physics laboratory. The U.S. interagency committee charged with developing American positions for COCOM vetoed the British application. The British then successfully appealed to President Nixon to reopen the case. The president received conflicting opinions, with some agencies led by the Defense Department opposing the sale and others, led by the State Department, supporting it. The president approved the sale, reportedly after being convinced that cheating would avail the Soviets relatively little (Wade, 1974).

Conclusions

The issue of technology transfer to the Soviet Union has prompted within the American decisionmaking process a spirited dialogue that seems to insure adequate consideration of all pertinent views and alternatives.

References

Tabor, John K. 1974. "Technology Exchange with the USSR: Achieving a Favorable Balance." *Research Management* 17:4 (July):9-12.

U.S. Congress, House of Representatives. 1974. Remarks of Rep. Ben Blackburn. *Congressional Record* (20 February): H 934.

Wade, Nicholas. 1974. "Computer Sales to U.S.S.R.: Critics Look for Quid pro Quos." *Science* 183:4124 (8 February):499-501.

17 Nuclear Reactors and Foreign Policy: Challenges of a Global Technology

Rodney L. Huff

On December 8, 1953, President Dwight D. Eisenhower proclaimed before the United Nations General Assembly that the United States was prepared to assist other countries around the world in developing national programs in the civil uses of atomic energy. This remarkable American offer had a twofold purpose. It was designed first of all to dramatize the peaceful side of the atom and to turn attention toward the profound uses to which atomic energy could be put, while lessening the almost total preoccupation with the destructive features of this new-found energy source that had characterized the postwar era up to that time. The speech was an exercise in Cold War statesmanship, and it established the United States as the world's leader in developing and applying the peaceful atom around the globe. The UN speech also typified the optimism with which the U.S. government has viewed atomic energy as a humanitarian force which it should share with all peoples.

The most striking facet of the peaceful applications of atomic energy is the generation of electric power by nuclear reactors. While projections in the early 1950s for the development of civilian nuclear power were somewhat overly optimistic, by the 1970s the door has begun to open on the era foreseen by President Eisenhower in 1953. There are today over 130 nuclear power reactors operating around the world and producing over 51,000 megawatts of electric power. By 1980, it is estimated, nuclear reactors will be producing 293,000 megawatts of electricity, and by 1990 current projections are for 1,232,000 megawatts.

The full implications of the broad policy statement enunciated by President Eisenhower are still unfolding. However, the global scope of civilian nuclear power development and the fact that all modern states consider an assured source of electric power to be a vital national interest leave no doubt as to why civilian nuclear power has increasingly become a subject of foreign policy concern. This chapter identifies the major foreign policy issues associated with the worldwide growth of civilian nuclear power.

Civilian nuclear power takes on foreign policy significance at three different levels. In one category are questions associated with what may be termed the "quality of life" or human level. Problems associated with the impact of new technologies on the individual have not traditionally fallen within the realm of foreign policy. However, because of the international commercial trade in nuclear reactors and fuels, the transportation of radioactive and toxic nuclear materials across national boundaries and on the high seas, the disposal and storage of waste materials, and the movement of nuclear-powered vessels in and out of foreign ports, foreign offices have been drawn into this entirely new genre of interstate relations.

Such questions are basically health and safety issues, and some of them are the subject of heated, and sometimes highly emotional, national debates. It would be wrong to suggest that they can be easily resolved. However, solutions are more a matter of degree than of direction. There is a common perception in all countries that there are dangers associated with nuclear fission. The objective is also clear: generating electric power as safely as possible. And there is a growing body of technical data and operating experience from which to draw. The debate is waged in terms of "how great are the dangers," "how safe is safe enough," and "which data are most relevant." In the foreign policy context, though, these issues do not develop into matters of clearcut national interest. Because of the common perception of the benefits of nuclear power—and of the dangers—and because there are no directly countervailing national interests involved, such questions would appear to be the most amenable to treatment by common action between governments.

There is a second set of issues, with growing foreign policy ramifications, that is associated with the safe and responsible operation of nuclear reactors. These fall into two distinct categories: safeguards and physical security. Safeguards refer to actual on-site inspections (and a host of related mechanical devices, records, and reports) designed to ensure that civilian power reactors are utilized by the responsible national authorities solely for the generation of electric power and to detect diversion to some unauthorized military-related use. Physical security refers to those measures instituted to protect reactors and nuclear fuel materials from theft, sabotage, or diversion by criminal elements or political dissidents. The International Atomic Energy Agency (IAEA), since its establishment in 1957, has increasingly taken on the responsibility of applying international safeguards. Physical security lies primarily in the hands of national authorities in individual states.

The IAEA safeguards program has been supported by countries of all political persuasions. However, the applicability of IAEA safeguards across-the-board is not universally accepted, and this represents one rather substantial hole in the safeguards net. Although the United States or some other country exporting a reactor or nuclear materials can condition that export on the application of safeguards in the recipient state, there is nothing to prohibit a non-nuclear weapon state, which is not a party to the Nuclear Non-Proliferation Treaty, from seeking to develop its own indigenous nuclear capabilities for whatever end use it may desire. It is this group of non-nuclear weapon, non-NPT states that represents the most serious proliferation problem and the most serious defect in the IAEA safeguards fabric. This critical group of states, a number of which are relatively well advanced in nuclear technology, takes varying attitudes toward the NPT. Some, including Japan and the EURATOM states, have indicated they will join. Others, including India, have said flatly they will not. The question of the extent to which the United States should encourage such states to become full NPT parties has been given added relevance by the recent Indian explosion of a nuclear device.

Although a fairly rigorous international safeguards regime has been developed and applied through the IAEA, nothing comparable has been accomplished in the area of physical security concerning effective protection of reactors and nuclear materials. Adequate security measures will become of increasing priority as the number of power reactors increases and the amount of radioactive, toxic, and weapons-useable materials being transported around the globe expands.

The pivotal question in establishing some sort of internationally observed physical security guidelines is to define the maximum credible threat. With the range of possible incidents running from a one-time, hit-and-run caper by smalltime local criminals to a well-coordinated and financed operation by highly trained and dedicated revolutionaries (possibly with formal governmental backing), it is possible to postulate a great number of scenarios. The nature of the threat and the most appropriate type of physical security countermeasures will vary from country to country.

Clearly, some sort of cooperative effort in policing the nuclear industry on an international level is in order. That a truly unified program could be built is questionable, however. The starting point would almost inevitably have to be individual police systems within each state, and the total effect may be mostly of an *ad hoc* nature. Such a disjointed situation need not necessarily be viewed as entirely negative, since flexibility will be the absolutely essential ingredient for whatever sort of international effort that may emerge.

There are generally well-defined perceptions of the international problems physical security systems, and safeguards as well, are designed to meet. Instituting physical arrangements and safeguards are fairly straightforward matters of technical competence. Nevertheless, the foreign policy implications of security and safeguards are crucial because they impinge so directly on the self-images of national sovereignty that states so firmly retain. These issues should prove to be one of the most active areas of foreign policy action both because of their urgent nature and because these issues are politically relevant on the level of international organizations, on the level of interstate relations, and on the national level simultaneously.

Finally, there is a third category of foreign policy issues, essentially political in nature, for which no clearcut alternative courses of action have been identified. Indeed, there is no sharp perception of the objectives that ought to be pursued, not even any agreement in common on the nature of the problems being faced. At the heart of the matter is the question of what impact the spread of peaceful nuclear technology will have on the international political system. The humanistic theory that international sharing of technology has an equalizing effect that mitigates the basic causes of instability among countries has a certain logic in the abstract. What the actual effect may be in any particular instance is much less certain. The issue is now squarely before us with the prospect of civilian nuclear reactors moving into developing countries—many of them in areas of actual or latent hostility. The total effect on balance is even more obscure since this technological input is merely one variable in a complex and changing matrix of political, economic, and social forces.

Of equal importance is the question of weaving a global fabric of rules and regulations within which the peaceful atom can be made to serve man in safety and security. A sense of common purpose among the major supplier states of nuclear materials and equipment is perhaps the most critical criterion. Unless those nations that control the fountainhead of technology share a common perception of their special responsibilities, efforts on a broader international front will be hobbled from the start. There is a growing awareness of the urgency of the problems at hand, but there is lacking generally the high-level commitment of political will essential for concerted policy initiatives.

The foreign policy issues associated with the worldwide growth of civilian nuclear power industries, and of peaceful uses of nuclear energy generally, have just recently begun to prick the imagination of a broad cross section of the foreign affairs community. Some excellent ground work has already been done. However, most conceptualizations of this interface between nuclear technology and foreign affairs have tended to establish certain technological givens and then postulate the likely or unlikely impact upon international political behavior. Of equal interest, and of more direct foreign policy impact, is to fix the course of one's investigation on the ultimate foreign policy objective and then manipulate the technological resources available in alternative patterns to that end. The challenges that face us in the last third of the twentieth century merit the best minds we can apply to them.

18 Foreign Policy Doctrines

William H. Overholt and Marylin Chou

Throughout most of American history, U.S. foreign policy has been guided by various succinct "doctrines": the "No Entangling Alliance" doctrine of Washington's Farewell Address, the Monroe Doctrine, the Open Door Policy, and the Truman Doctrine. Likewise, the basic foreign policy principles of foreign states can usually be summarized in a few concise slogans analogous to American doctrines. From "Carthago delenda est" in Cato's Rome to "Self-Reliance" in contemporary China, the foreign policy doctrine has proved a useful form of expression.

The simplicity with which policy doctrines are typically stated leads some observers to dismiss them as banal—as minor forms of public relations—but close examination reveals evidence that policymakers regard them as important. Presidents repeatedly appeal to doctrines to justify current difficult decisions; for instance, in 1962 and 1965 Presidents Kennedy and Johnson appealed to the Monroe Doctrine of 1823, to justify decisions on Cuba and the Dominican Republic. National security bureaucracies spend substantial money and time interpreting doctrines and drawing detailed policy conclusions. Recent presidents and their supporters have consistently, but unsuccessfully, attempted to elevate their policies to the status of "doctrines." Examples are the so-called Eisenhower, Kennedy, and Johnson Doctrines, all of which were only rhetorical variations on the Truman Doctrine, and the Nixon Doctrine, which significantly altered the Truman Doctrine but lacked the stature to replace it. The omnipresence of foreign policy doctrines and their analogues suggests they possess some fundamental importance.

Doctrines are typically unilateral declarations of policy designed to elicit domestic public support, to serve as axiomatic policy guidelines for domestic decisionmakers and bureaucrats, and to announce basic policy to foreign governments. These purposes, and especially the first two, explain the principal characteristics of doctrines discussed below.

Simplicity, Conciseness, and Lucidity

Statements intended to serve as axiomatic guides to policy must by definition be simple, concise, and lucid statements of purpose or strategy.

149

Simplicity at this level facilitates complexity and nuance in the elaboration of subordinate policies—as one can easily perceive by trying to imagine an arithmetic based on complex, convoluted axioms. The audiences toward which policy doctrines are targeted reinforce these requirements for simplicity, conciseness, and lucidity. It has long been a rule of thumb for experienced administrators that huge bureaucracies cannot balance more than a few policy imperatives. Likewise, students of political movements have emphasized the necessity of goals that are understandable, visible, and simple (e.g., Weber, 1947, p. 427; Lipset, 1968, pp. 64, 83). Simple slogans like "Restore the Emperor" and "Liberté, Égalité, Fraternité" can mobilize mass public support in Tokugawa Japan or revolutionary France, whereas complicated analyses would be ignored. To mobilize mass support for foreign policy, equally clear invocations (to avoid entangling alliances, to defend free people, to remain self-reliant, to export in order to live) are required.

Abstractness and Flexibility

Doctrines rarely dictate the details of subordinate policies and decisions; instead, they provide flexible abstract contexts for subordinate policies. Thus, the Truman Doctrine of providing support for free peoples threatened by communism provided no detailed guidance for designers of NATO or the Marshall Plan or for U.S. presidents confronted by Soviet challenges in Berlin. But the doctrine does provide an overall rationale and cohesion for decisions.

All enduring doctrines are subject to serious reinterpretation and variation of emphasis as domestic and foreign exigencies change. Thus, for instance, the Monroe Doctrine began as a doctrine of nonintervention; then with the Roosevelt Corollary in 1904, it became a rationale for U.S. intervention. In 1928 the Corollary was repudiated, and subsequently the emphases of the Doctrine have continued to vary greatly. Such flexibility and abstractness are necessary characteristics of doctrines—first, because doctrines serve as axiomatic statements in a complex world; second, because a doctrine is expected to guide policy over long periods of time and therefore through diverse historical exigencies; and third, because doctrines appeal for support from a broad and amorphous public with many conflicting interests and attitudes. In other words, doctrines are abstract and flexible because they must be simple and yet cope with complexity, change, and diversity of opinion.

The abstractness and flexibility of doctrines draw the unwary observer toward two fallacies. First is the view that doctrines are banal public relations devices of little significance. But as noted above, they are banal only in the sense that all axioms, all ultimate principles, are banal. They are self-evident only *after* they have been tested and annealed by history.[a] Since they succeed or fail and since they can become disastrously obsolete (cf. Overholt, 1974)—as the "No Entangling Alliances" doctrine did in the late 1930s—they are not trivialities. Second is the view that doctrines have continuity only in name—that is, because of drastic reinterpretations there was not one Monroe Doctrine, but many; not one Open Door Policy, but many. But in every case, despite flexibility and abstraction, the major American doctrines have retained a core of hard meaning; despite varying interpretations, the Monroe Doctrine has continuously prohibited firm European assertions of hegemony over South American states.

Balance among Conflicting Principles

Doctrines are above all declarations of purpose, and only under rather special circumstances do a nation's foreign policy objectives become so simplified that they can be summarized in a single coherent sentence such as "Carthago delenda est" or "No entangling alliances" or commitment "to support free peoples who are resisting subjugation." In these situations, a single overwhelming fear (of Carthage, of foreign intervention, of Soviet expansion) has come to dominate policy. In "normal" situations where policy is not dominated by a single overwhelming fear, doctrines state two or three principles that may appear contradictory. The Open Door Policy, which dominated U.S. relations with Asia for two generations, demanded equal access to the China market, supported China's territorial integrity, and acknowledged that the United States would do little to support these principles.[b] The latter point did not contradict the others; it merely qualified them. Likewise the promise of the Nixon Doctrine to honor U.S. commitments did not contradict its later insistence on relying on local manpower; it merely qualified the commitment in some cases (e.g., Thailand) and reflected confidence that local manpower would prove adequate in others (e.g., Taiwan). The men who cried "Liberty, Equality, Fraternity" were not contradicting themselves; they were stating their values. That tradeoffs exist is understood. To mention them in a doctrine would be to transform the doctrine from invocation to analysis.

---

[a] Note that, despite their acknowledged brilliance in foreign affairs, Secretary Kissinger and President Nixon failed in their Nixon Doctrine to deal with ends as well as means, failed to provide a balanced view of their policies, and failed utterly to provide inspiration and clarity. Their brilliance was adequate to discern an historical turning point and the need for a new doctrine, inadequate to discern the nature of the turning point and to enunciate inspiring and enduring purposes for the new era.

[b] Historians have generally dwelt upon the first two parts of this policy, but the third was stated with equal clarity, and understood and acted upon by policymakers.

In addition to these basic characteristics, which derive from the axiomatic character of doctrines and from the needs of doctrines' audiences, doctrines exhibit a distinctive life cycle (Overholt, 1974). Initially some crisis, often a relatively minor one, forces policymakers to cut through the inertia and incrementalism of everyday decisions and enunciate a fundamental principle. The Open Door Policy responded to a series of mini-crises in U.S. relations with China, Britain, and Japan; the Truman Doctrine to limited crises in Greece and Turkey; the Monroe Doctrine to erroneous fears of French-Spanish intrigue; the "No Entangling Alliance" Doctrine to feared involvement in the European turmoil over the French revolution; the Nixon Doctrine to Vietnam.

But if an aspiring doctrine merely responds well to a single crisis, history forgets it. Successful doctrines are those tied directly to the great historical relationships of an entire era: to U.S. ascendance and European decline in Latin America (the Monroe Doctrine); to the peculiar and awesome power of the United States when her allies were still lost in the ashes after World War II (the Truman Doctrine); or to the trembling weakness of a young America in a world of European giants ("No Entangling Alliances"). Sometimes doctrines must even wait for history to catch up with them; the Monroe Doctrine of 1823 came to center stage only in the British-Venezuelan dispute by 1895. Thus, doctrines transcend their origins, and a response to Greek and Turkish problems becomes a worldwide policy for a generation.

Once formulated and found consistent with historical relationships, doctrines become institutionalized. Bureaucracies become restructured to implement the doctrines; for instance, the Japanese Ministry of International Trade and Industry was designed to stimulate exports and retard imports, in response to the doctrine of "We have to export in order to live," and persisted in these purposes even when they had become counterproductive. Individual reputations become tied to the policies. Major social groups and even the intellectual community reach near-consensus on policy axioms and penalize continued skepticism with sanctions ranging from urbane disagreement to McCarthyite attacks. Policy analysis becomes focused on incremental rather than synoptic issues, on means rather than ends. Legal and other commitments are made, so that altering the doctrine causes crises of credibility. The great abstractness and flexibility of doctrines inhibit perception that historical changes have rendered the doctrine obsolete. As a result, the world of the doctrine and the real world of history diverge until a new crisis (World War II, Vietnam, Japan's 1972 currency crisis) forces a reexamination of basic purpose and strategy. Then the cycle begins anew.

Doctrines or their analogues are requirements for integrated policy and public support. But vices accompany their virtues. For impoverished minds simplicity brings rigidity rather than flexibility. For political opponents balance appears self-contradictory. For perceptive individuals who foresee the obsolescence of a doctrine and for nations that employ obsolete doctrines, the doctrines' institutional inertia brings tragedy. To borrow Thomas Kuhn's terms from another field, a foreign policy paradigm is necessary, but eventually conceptual revolution becomes necessary.

References

Lipset, Seymour Martin. 1968. *Agrarian Socialism*. New York: Doubleday.

Overholt, William H. 1974. "From the Politics of Weakness to the Politics of Strength." *Orbis* 18:1 (Spring): 27-49.

Weber, Max. 1947. *The Theory of Social and Economic Organization*, translated by A.M. Henderson and Talcott Parsons. New York: Oxford University Press.

Index

155

About the Contributors

Sheldon Appleton is Professor of Political Science at Oakland University in Michigan. A one-time U.S. Foreign Service Officer and a University of Minnesota Ph.D., he has written books on U.S.-China policy and on U.S. foreign policy, and articles on foreign policy and Chinese political culture for such journals as *Asian Survey, International Studies Quarterly, China Quarterly, Pacific Affairs*, and the *Journal of Asian Studies*. His research deals with sources of presidential popularity and the structure of representation in the Japanese National Diet.

William O. Chittick, who received the Ph.D. from the Johns Hopkins University, is Associate Professor of Political Science at the University of Georgia. Besides articles in the *Journal of Politics* and elsewhere, he is the author of *State Department, Press and Pressure Groups*, and editor of *The Analysis of Foreign Policy Outputs*.

Marylin Chou is a member of the research staff of the Hudson Institute, Croton-on-Hudson, N.Y. Her research is in the areas of worldwide food problems and prospects, resource issues and vulnerabilities, and the economic development of the Middle East as part of a study treating world issues and trends. Mrs. Chou received the B.A. degree in political science from Wellesley College.

Stephen J. Cimbala is Associate Professor of Political Science and Associate Director for Academic Affairs at the Delaware County Campus, Pennsylvania State University. He received the Ph.D. from the University of Wisconsin, Madison. His contributions have included articles in the *American Political Science Review, World Politics*, and *Theory and Decision* (co-author). He edited a special issue of *Policy Sciences* (December 1973) on "Policy Sciences and Foreign Policy: Process and Outcome."

Kenneth Entin is Associate Professor of Political Science at California State College, Stanislaus. He received the Ph.D. from New York University. His studies on congressional committee decisionmaking have appeared in the *Western Political Quarterly* and the *Journal of Political and Military Sociology*. A monograph on the California Department of Consumer Affairs was published by the Institute of Governmental Affairs, University of California, Davis. Dr. Entin is continuing his research on legislative behavior.

Ernst W. Gohlert is Associate Professor of Political Science at Eastern Washington State College, after returning from a research year at the Deutsche Gesellschaft für Auswärtige Politik in Bonn. He is completing a book on German foreign policy and national security organization. Professor Gohlert received the Ph.D. from Washington State University, and has written recently on security issues, including an article in *Comparative Defense Policy*, edited by Frank B. Horton et al.

David E. Griffith, a doctoral candidate at the University of Illinois at Urbana-Champaign, is preparing a dissertation on military construction policymaking in the United States. He has recently joined the research staff of the Illinois Commission on Intergovernmental Relations to work in the area of health policy planning.

Charles F. Hermann is Professor of Political Science and Associate Director of the Mershon Center at The Ohio State University. After completing the Ph.D. at Northwestern University, he taught at Princeton University, was an International Fellow of the Council on Foreign Relations, and served as a staff member of the National Security Council. In addition to numerous scholarly articles, he has written *Crisis in Foreign Policy* and edited *International Crises*. He founded the CREON (Comparative Research on the Events of Nations) data bank.

Rodney L. Huff is a Foreign Service Officer with the U.S. Department of State, and worked on the staff of the Department's Office of Atomic Energy Affairs in 1973-1974. He received the Ph.D. from The George Washington University where he wrote a dissertation on political decisionmaking in the Japanese atomic energy program. He is serving in the Office of the Science Counselor at the U.S. Embassy in Tokyo.

Jerry B. Jenkins is Assistant Professor of Political Science at the University of Georgia, where he is engaged in an extensive NSF-funded project developing contextually-based indicators of international interaction.

Thomas H. Karas is Adjunct Assistant Professor of International Relations in the Boston University Graduate School Overseas Program and is now teaching in Vicenza, Italy. He received the Ph.D. from Harvard University. He has been working on a book on the uses and effects of deception in the conduct of the Vietnam War and in the conduct of foreign policy in general.

Lawrence Korb is Professor of Management at the Naval War College and an Adjunct Scholar of the American Enterprise Institute for Public Policy

Research. He received the Ph.D. from the State University of New York at Albany and is the author or coauthor of numerous articles and books on national security policy and the defense budget. He is preparing for publication a book on the *Joint Chiefs of Staff* and one on *Pentagon Politics*.

William H. Overholt, Ph.D., Yale University, is on the Research Staff of the Hudson Institute, Croton-on-Hudson, New York, where he has coordinated and authored major studies, including "The World, 1982-1991" and "The United States and Asia in the Seventies." In 1975-1976 he is Senior Fellow at Columbia University's Research Institute on International Change. His articles have appeared in *Southeast Asia Quarterly, Orbis, Pacific Community,* and *Asian Survey*.

Don C. Piper is Professor of Government and Politics at the University of Maryland. He is the author of one book on international law and a contributor to several other volumes on international legal matters. In addition he has published a number of articles in scholarly journals, including the *American Journal of International Law, Journal of Conflict Resolution,* and *Georgia Journal of International and Comparative Law*. He is pursuing additional research on the relationship between international law and foreign policy.

Elmer Plischke, Professor and former Head (1954-1968) of the Department of Government and Politics at the University of Maryland, received the Ph.D. at Clark University (1943). He is the author and compiler of some twenty books and monographs—including *Conduct of American Diplomacy, Summit Diplomacy: Personal Diplomacy of the President of the United States, Systems of Integrating the International Community, Foreign Relations Decision-Making: Options Analysis*, and *United States Diplomats and Their Missions: A Profile of American Diplomatic Emissaries since 1778*—as well as sixty articles and essays published in the *American Journal of International Law, American Political Science Review, Foreign Service Journal, International Studies Quarterly, Journal of Politics, Orbis, Political Science Quarterly, World Affairs*, and other professional and literary journals. He served as a member (1967-1972) and Chairman (1969-1970) of the Department of State Advisory Committee on "Foreign Relations."

Aline Olson Quester is Assistant Professor of Economics at the State University of New York, Cortland, and is completing the Ph.D. dissertation at Tufts University on the impact of tax incentives on female participation in the labor force.

George H. Quester is Professor of Government at Cornell University. He received the Ph.D. from Harvard University and is the author of several books on defense policy.

Barry S. Rundquist is Assistant Professor of Political Science at the University of Illinois at Urbana-Champaign. He received the Ph.D. from Stanford University. His research, which has appeared in the *American Political Science Review* and elsewhere, concerns the structure of policymaking in Congress and military procurement spending.

Ralph Sanders is Professor of Public Administration at the Industrial College of the Armed Forces and Adjunct Professor at The American University. He received the Ph.D. from Georgetown University. The author of *Project Plowshare: The Peaceful Uses of Nuclear Explosions* (1962) and *The Politics of Defense Analysis* (1974) and the editor of four anthologies, he has also contributed articles to scholarly journals and magazines such as *Orbis, Technology and Culture, Military Review, Perspectives in Defense Management*, and *The Bulletin of the Atomic Scientists*. He specializes in the field of science, technology, and government, with emphasis on international relations. At the present time he is preparing an anthology, *Science and Technology: Vital National Resources*, to appear in late 1975.

Richard N. Swift, Professor of Politics, New York University, is completing a biography of the British League of Nations champion, Lord Robert Cecil. He is the author of *World Affairs and the College Curriculum* and *International Law: Current and Classic*. He has been a visiting lecturer at Harvard and Yale universities, and serves on executive committees of the International Law Association-American Branch and the Commission to Study the Organization of Peace.

About the Editor

Richard L. Merritt is Professor of Political Science and Communications at the University of Illinois at Urbana-Champaign, and directs the University's Office of West European Studies. After receiving the Ph.D. from Yale University, he has worked in the fields of international communications, quantitative cross-national research, and political integration, with special reference to Berlin and Germany.